SIMPLE WORDS

John XXIII

SIMPLE WORDS

Introduced by
Loris Capovilla

ST PAULS

Original Title: *Parole Semplici*

Copyright © ÀNCORA S.r.l. 2000

ÀNCORA EDITRICE
Via G.B. Niccolini, 8 – 20154 Milano, Italy

Translated by Andrew Tulloch

ST PAULS Publishing
187 Battersea Bridge Road, London SW11 3AS, UK

English Translation Copyright © ST PAULS (UK) 2003

ISBN 085439 662 4

Distributed in Australia and New Zealand by
ST PAULS PUBLICATIONS
PO Box 906, Strathfield NSW 2135, Australia

Set by TuKan DTP, Fareham, Hampshire, UK
Printed by Biddles Ltd., Guildford, UK

ST PAULS is an activity of the priests and brothers
of the Society of St Paul who proclaim the Gospel
through the media of social communication

CONTENTS

Allow me to humbly introduce myself.
Like every other person on earth,
I come from a particular family and place.
I have been blessed with good physical health,
and enough common sense
to grasp things quickly and clearly;
I also have an inclination to love people
which keeps me faithful to the law of the Gospel,
and respectful of my own rights and those of others.
It stops me from doing harm to anyone;
it encourages me to do good to all.
I come from a modest family,
and was brought up in contented and blessed poverty,
a poverty that has few needs,
that protects the highest virtues and makes them grow,
and prepares one for the great adventure of life.

Pope John XXIII

NOTE

This anthology of John XXIII's thoughts has been taken from the speeches which the Pope gave in the last ten years of his life, from his nomination as Patriarch of Venice on 15 January 1953 until his death on 3 June 1963, and from *Journal of a Soul*, his spiritual diary, which begins in 1895 and ends during the last days of his life.

The dates which accompany each thought correspond to the date when the speech from which it is taken was given. When the date is preceded by the abbreviation *JS*, this means that the thought comes from *Journal of a Soul*.

INTRODUCTION

Philip answered Jesus, 'Six months' wages would not buy enough bread for each of them to get a little.' One of his disciples, Andrew, Simon Peter's brother, said to him, 'There is a boy here who has five barley loaves and two fish. But what are they among so many people?'

(Jn 6:7-9)

I can almost see him approaching Jesus, this young man, light as an angel, smiling and full of trepidation, radiant with interior light. His eyes gaze into those of the Divine Master. His heart beats with that of Jesus. A few moments of silence, contemplation and prayer; then the miracle of the multiplication of loaves and fishes.

This young man is the prototype of those men and women who in the course of the centuries made themselves instruments of the Lord's miracles, offering themselves and all that they had for the annunciation of the kingdom, with boundless faith, determined to work with him in building a community where the lamps of faith, of service, and of love shine forth.

The Gospel account is simple and sublime, just as anyone who allows themselves to be penetrated by the light will reach to the sublime themselves and radiate the light around them without needing to say anything.

During the course of his long life, Angelo Giuseppe Roncalli, who through this anthology of the 'wisdom of the heart' converses with us, continually repeated the gesture of the young man from Galilee: he gave to Jesus all that he had, intelligence and sensibility, work and prayer; his time, his innocence, his simplicity.

Simplicity above all, which is the very height of human and Christian virtue and which presupposes the harmonious presence of all the other virtues in the same person.

John XXIII affirmed the presence of simplicity in his life during the first days of his pontificate, when the chroniclers and those who have opinions were watching to discover who he was and what was so extraordinary about him to give rise to such an immediate and vast groundswell of sympathy and approval: 'This is the mystery of my life. Do not look for other explanations. I have always repeated St Gregory Nazianzen's words: "The will of God is our peace."'

In all he did John XXIII moved continually within the well marked-out ambit of doing God's will and listening to his word: from the short stretch of road that separates Sotto il Monte from Carvico, which the young Angelo took at the age of nine years in order to learn the foundations of grammar and logical analysis; from his service in the diocese of Bergamo; from his sojourns at Rome, in the Middle East, at Paris and Venice, until his final berth on the banks of the Tiber. He did this with the calm certainty of having remained faithful to the tasks and commissions entrusted to him and to the divine illumination that he obtained from the third book of the *Imitation of Christ*, which brought him to the land of interior peace and true liberty:

> Seek, child, to do the will of others rather than your own. Always choose to have less rather than more. Look always for the last place and seek to be beneath all others. Always wish and pray that the will of God be fully carried out in you.
>
> (Book III, Chapter 23)

The Pope's life was one of unfailing and complete obedience, obedience that he clearly understood. He lived it joyfully, to the point that he could take pleasure in it on the threshold of his 80th birthday, offering us a lesson which is always timely and of which we have need:

Everyone must be treated with respect, prudence and evangelical simplicity. It is commonly believed and considered fitting that even the everyday language of the Pope should be full of mystery and awe. But the example of Jesus is more closely followed in the most appealing simplicity, not dissociated from the God-given prudence of wise and holy men. Simplicity may cause, I don't say scorn, but a lack of consideration on the part of those who think themselves wise. But such people are of no account; even if their opinions and conduct inflict some humiliations, no notice should be taken of them at all: in the end everything ends in their defeat and confusion. The 'simplex et rectus ac timens', 'simple, upright, God-fearing man' (Job 1:1), is always the worthiest and the strongest. Naturally he must always be sustained by a wise and gracious prudence. He is a simple man who is not ashamed to profess the Gospel, even in the face of those who consider it to be nothing but weakness and childish nonsense, and who professes it entirely, on all occasions, and in the presence of all; he does not let himself be deceived or prejudiced by his fellows, nor does he lose his peace of soul, however they may treat him.

Simple Words – a small book with a big message – gives witness to a noble and holy life, unties complicated knots, presents clearly all the precious pearls of John XXIII's teaching, and encourages us to return and meditate once again on John Chrysostom's warning, whose words the Pope of 'simplicity of heart and of lips' made resound at the start of his pontificate:

> Christ has left us on the earth so that we might become lighthouses that illuminate, doctors that teach. Let us fulfil our task like angels, like those who bring news to humankind. So doing we will become adults among children, spiritual people among the carnal with the aim of winning them for God; we will become seed and bear much fruit. It would not even be necessary to expound doctrine if our conduct were sufficiently radiant; and it would not be necessary to use words if our works were to give sufficient witness. There would be no more pagans, if we were to behave like true Christians.
>
> (Homily on the first letter of St Paul to Timothy)

† LORIS FRANCESCO CAPOVILLA

God

GOD OUR FATHER

And because you are children,
God has sent
the Spirit of his Son into our hearts,
crying, Abba! Father!

(Gal 4:6)

1 The sun is always above: God who shines and watches over us. (19 July 1961)

2 The great poem of the life and the history of the whole of humankind finds resonance in, and is entirely contained within, the 'Our Father'.

(4 November 1961)

3 Behold the 'Our Father', the prayer taught us by Jesus, the prayer which sums up the entire Gospel.

(11 September 1960)

4 The first thing that I would ask is that everywhere the holy name of God be respected, blessed, and given honour. Alas, how many Christians do not honour their own baptism, using certain expressions of impatience and of anger! (11 September 1960)

5 We ask the Lord that his kingdom come. It is a kingdom of peace, and not of violence; there is no abuse of power, and no revolt against the fundamental laws of the human spirit; a kingdom of love, of forgiveness, of justice – of a justice that is higher than the earthly order of justice, since this latter has recourse to the use of arms, even though this may be in the strictly necessary case of self-defence.

(11 September 1960)

6 When one speaks of the Kingdom of God, one must not mistakenly identify it with the political structures of human power, as often happened in history, and as happens here and there even in our own day – structures which are themselves visible expressions of human arrogance.   (28 October 1959)

7 The third petition of the 'Our Father' asks that the Lord's will be done. Yes, in all and at all times, amidst the difficulties of life, in the muddle of our daily disagreements: through poverty, through illness, right up until death. Yes, the will of God is our peace.
(28 January 1958)

8 Bread, like the water we drink and the air that we breathe, is the sign of the true brotherhood and sisterhood of humankind; it has its origins in the fatherhood of God, and expresses itself in the common use of his gifts.   (20 September 1961)

9 For every sin there is forgiveness. The world is still going strong, as it always has done, because the voice and the blood of Christ implore for mercy and pity.
(28 October 1959)

10 All is forgiven to the person who knows how to grant forgiveness themselves, and has a desire to do so. And all is made beautiful in the person who has, or obtains anew, a pure and innocent soul and expresses it in fairness, justice and brotherhood, in true Christian brotherhood.   (28 October 1959)

11 God forgives the sins committed against his divine majesty: but he does not forgive sins committed by those brothers and sisters in whom forgiveness is lacking.   (15 September 1958)

12 The divine prayer that Jesus taught us on the mountain – the prayer through which we lift up our daily lives to him, the starting point which helps to form our minds – is based on a cry of utter abandonment to God omnipotent, that he save us from the 'evil one': 'Deliver us from evil' (Mt 16:3).

(28 October 1959)

13 Unfortunately, 'the whole world lies under the power of the evil one' (1 Jn 5:19). We can count on God to come to our aid and to show us mercy in order that we may be kept safe from the great misfortune of falling under his power: but our cooperation is required, a firm will to keep ourselves from evil and from the one who suggests it and inspires it. (28 October 1959)

14 God can be defined as, among other things, 'mercy': a profoundly human name, since it has been completely filled with the grace of Jesus: the true name of salvation, of repose amidst ups and downs of life which are so often painful: light to our eyes, relief in our tiredness, the security of eternal peace.

(18 June 1957)

15 Our heavenly Father is so good that he listens not only to the pleadings of those who speak to him, but also knows how to read the hearts of those whose lips are silent. (24 September 1959)

16 We are in the Lord's good hands, and he watches over us and sustains us. (3 July 1962)

17 The Lord thinks of everything: of the sun that rises and the sun that is hidden; of sad days and days filled with peace. Life is long; and even if, for some, it is not very extensive, there are many things which do change, and there are many unforeseen interventions, which help us to see that Providence is at work.

(11 September 1960)

18 We must do everything we can to open ourselves to the rain which comes from on high. If we do this we will be able to accept the inspirations that come from God our Father and to carry our crosses with a joyful soul and the acceptance of God's will, since without the Cross we will make no progress.

(13 March 1963)

19 Thanks to our prayers and our sacrifices, Divine Providence is able to bring about one of the greatest mysteries of history: the mystery of the Lord's mercy towards all people. (13 July 1959)

20 Not only the Christian family, but also the family of the whole universe is the creation and work of God, and depends on him. (19 December 1962)

21 We must abandon ourselves to Providence, trusting and believing in it, as a child trusts and believes in its mother. (24 September 1959)

22 Everything, therefore, can be of use to us: everything from heaven, from earth, from past history, from the conditions of the present day, and from all that is happening around us. Everything can help add a little sweetness to life, and in so doing lift us up to the Author of life himself, towards him to whom we owe everything. (10 January 1959)

23 Open your hearts to your Heavenly Father and allow the pleasant and gracious odour of your gratitude to ascend to his throne. (15 August 1959)

CHRIST OUR BROTHER

Those whom he foreknew
he also predestined
to be conformed to the image of his Son,
in order that he might be the firstborn
of many children.

(Rom 8:29)

24 In the beginning was the Word. All things came into being through him, and without him not one thing came into being. The Word became flesh and dwelt among us (cf Jn 1:1-14). This is the sacred page, the most precious page ever written.   (25 July 1957)

25 Behold the very highest peak and the guide of all history: Christ. 'The Word became flesh and dwelt among us'.   (10 August 1959)

26 The coming of Jesus at Christmas established, in flesh and blood, the first contact of divinity with humanity, and effected the first transfusion between the two. Through this humanity received new life and was lifted up towards its final and eternal glorification.
(25 July 1957)

27 Among all the peaks which as Christians and human beings we can ascend, the very highest is to be sought here: direct contact with Jesus through his body and blood.   (1 April 1956)

28 Through Christ his Son, through the Church who is faithful to her spouse of blood, the heavenly Father continues to converse with the world, to fill it with the supreme truth that is his very essence.
(25 December 1957)

29 In Christ salvation is brought about for all people, all being wounded by sin. This is the great and sure point of reference amidst the darkness of doctrinal error and moral aberration: the human person, through the Word of God who became flesh, is now brought into the life of the blessed Trinity and inherits heaven; serenity and peace enter into human life and temper its trials and difficulties. (13 February 1961)

30 In seeing Jesus, omnipotent yet humble, infinite yet poor, Word of God yet silent, all behold the salvation which comes from God. And so, taking heart, let us try to render the mysterious and grace-filled passage that is our human existence more worthy: for our own good, more meritorious; and for the good of our fellow creatures, of greater benefit to them. (25 December 1961)

31 With the Incarnation the human journey towards the heavenly homeland received a fresh start, and humanity is now elevated to the lofty status of being coheirs of heaven; and from the hidden life there rises a canticle of praise to the dignity and greatness of the family, in praise of the sacred duty of work and of its nobility. (4 January 1962)

32 Jesus and his Gospel are the great point of contradiction in the history of the human race. (15 June 1956)

33 The prayer of Christ is light of morning, security in the hours of toil and uncertainty, and confidence during the hours of evening and of night. (4 January 1959)

34 Either with Christ, each person shouldering some light cross, or without him, lost in uncertainty, risk, disorder, in the all-encompassing abyss.

(28 October 1959)

35 The one way along which we will not get lost, the one truth which cannot lead us into error, the one life that does not lead to death, is and always will be, Christ. (1 October 1959)

36 We must never be afraid of Christ, but have only the fullest and most unlimited trust in him.

(11 November 1962)

37 Jesus' eyes are full of tenderness and authority; his word is truth; his hand rises gently to indicate the correct path to all, the way of good discipline that helps all work together and directs their efforts to the common good. (10 August 1962)

38 Without Jesus, without a living faith, a joyful hope, and active charity in him and through him, your life would lose all meaning, it would become as obscure as the Plain of Lombardy when it is shrouded by the falling snows. (2 June 1962)

39 At the very foundation of everything, yesterday as today, stands Christ – the beginning and the end – the Alpha and Omega of all science and civilisation.

(10 September 1955)

40 Human history began with a bloody episode: the killing of a brother. The law of love, which the Creator stamped on the human heart, was lacerated by an evil will that at once led humanity down the paths of injustice. Unity was shattered and nothing less was required than the intervention of the Son of God himself. The Son undertook out of obedience to restore the holy bonds which had linked the human family, but which had been put under great pressure from the outset. (23 December 1958)

41 To the eye of faith trials are regarded as a necessary cross, a powerful aid to living and acting well, a clear witness to the fact that if Christ died on the cross he desires that we be near him, and that he calls to us and awaits us. There he welcomes us, since the Cross is the mark of the glorification in which we ourselves will participate. (26 February 1963)

42 Our Lord Jesus Christ, when he offered himself as the immaculate and peaceful victim on the altar of the Cross, brought humankind back to the heavenly Father's embrace and opened up the paths of true progress that raise human civilisations up and make them holy. (28 October 1962)

43 This cry for compassion and mercy, that Christ repeated through his drops of blood, 'with loud cries and tears' (Heb 5:7), finds its answer in the invitation issued by the same Divine Redeemer to the mutual forgiveness between brothers and sisters and to the true triumph. True triumph we say, not illusion, deception, or corruption – but the true triumph of forgiveness and peace. (28 October 1959)

44 Christ is before you, dead for your sake. Go and partake of the precious drops of his Blood in the Sacrament of his love and then, in the most intimate aspects of your life, in your various activities, be they social, professional or domestic, in all the places you frequent, with all the people you come in contact with, you will give honour to Our Lord Jesus Christ, who brought forgiveness down upon earth.

(17 April 1963)

45 My great book, from which henceforth I must learn with greater care and love the lessons of divine wisdom, is the crucifix.   (*JS*, 10 April 1903)

46 Christ is risen, alleluia! The greeting announces a project of great radiance: life instead of death; peace instead of divisions; charity instead of egoism; the truth instead of lies; and instead of that which depresses, the triumph of the light, of purity and mutual respect.

(14 April 1963)

47 Beside the risen Christ you will feel the fragrance of his body and of his divine blood through the very warmth of his life.   (1 April 1956)

48 Do not desire to be conformed outwardly to this present age: it is ephemeral and passing. But desire to be transformed into that which is always new, that is, Christ.   (23 February 1955)

49 May you be clothed in Christ, as much in the silence of your heart as in your words and conduct. May you be decorated with Christ, with his modesty, gentleness, prudence, love, patience in times of trial, sweetness, seriousness, and constancy. Take off the old person. Put on Christ, act for Christ, be Christ.

(24 September 1959)

50 Jesus is present in the Church in the person of his Vicar, in the living repetition of the Gospel teaching, and in the pouring out of his Blood through the Sacrament of his love.   (24 September 1959)

51 Christ is present in every soul, and there he has his dwelling of grace and truth. Christ alone can save the world; with Mary leading us by the hand, we will surely reach the one who is our peace and our happiness.   (25 March 1962)

52 Make the person and the teaching of Jesus Christ central to your life.   (27 June 1962)

53 'I am the light of the world'; 'I am the way, the truth, and the life' (Jn 8:12; 14:6). These words and all that they signify have a divine seal placed on them by words which close Matthew's Gospel: 'And remember, I am with you always, to the end of the age' (Mt 28:20).   (14 November 1960)

54 O Prince of Peace, Risen Jesus, look with kindness on the whole of humanity. And humanity looks to you alone for help and for the healing of its wounds. In the days of your earthly life, you showed a special love for little ones, the unimportant, and the suffering; you always went in search of sinners. Grant that all may call upon you, and find you, that they might have truth and life in you who are life. O Lamb sacrificed for our salvation, may we always have your peace: Lamb of God who takes away the sins of the world, grant us peace.   (13 April 1963)

THE SPIRIT OUR STRENGTH

When the Spirit of truth comes,
he will guide you into all the truth;
for he will not speak on his own,
but will speak whatever he hears,
and he will declare to you the things that are to come.

(Jn 16:13)

55 The Holy Spirit, who formed the body of Christ in the womb of the Virgin Mary, forms and brings together, heals and strengthens those who belong to Christ. (27 June 1960)

56 When the grace of the Lord takes possession of a soul, it transfigures it. (15 August 1962)

57 When the Holy Spirit blazes it is like a fiery river which is poured on all those who belong to the Church, making their hearts firm and binding them together in a sacred pact of mutual love and charity.

(29 August 1957)

58 Let us allow this transforming fire to penetrate us, as the Apostles did on the day of Pentecost! It will burn away the dross that our nature, afflicted by sin, inevitably collects. (20 October 1960)

59 On this earth we are never alone. There is one who accompanies us and offers help that is without compare. (30 May 1962)

60 Jesus assures us that the Holy Spirit will continue to cause a most wonderful supernatural fruitfulness to spring forth in the Church, a fruitfulness that places in the hearts of virgins, martyrs and confessors the seeds of those heroic virtues which are characteristic of sanctity. (20 August 1957)

61 The Spirit of Jesus brightens up the harsher side of life, sweetens all the difficulties that seem to multiply through of the events of each day and the various troubles we experience, and propels us to forgiveness, understanding, and love. (28 October 1960)

62 The Holy Spirit is the life of the Church that never grows old. The Spirit makes blossom a spring that never knows winter. In the midst of anxieties and troubles the Spirit prepares and accomplishes a victory that is unfailing and sure. (27 June 1960)

63 The Spirit is always at work in the depths of every soul, inspiring them, in order to render the Church that Jesus built once and for all through the sacrifice of his blood, pure, spotless, and without blemish, worthy to be presented to his Father on the day of the final triumph. (20 August 1957)

64 Only the Holy Spirit can inflame our spirits with the desire to be virtuous, and preserve them from the contamination of sin. (27 April 1959)

65 We should listen well to the Divine Guest who accompanies us, and walks with us along the path of time. (21 January 1962)

66 O Holy Spirit the Paraclete, bring to completion the work that Jesus began in us. Make our prayer strong and unceasing; hasten the day when we will have a profound inner life. Let no earthy bond prevent us from doing justice to our vocation; let no affairs of ours, through our sloth, compromise the demands of justice; let none of our schemings reduce the immense dimensions of charity to the narrow confines of our tiny egoisms. Let all that we are and do, be large.

(10 June 1962)

Mary

MOTHER

When Jesus saw his mother
and the disciple whom he loved standing beside her,
he said to his mother, 'Woman, here is your son.'
Then he said to the disciple, 'Here is your mother.'

(Jn 19:26-27)

67 For those who believe in Our Lord Jesus Christ, for those who belong to his Holy Church: here is your Mother: Mary! (7 September 1960)

68 Mary is ever present in our thoughts: and this most excellent Mother helps each one of her children as they go through their lives. She helps us to achieve the aim of every life here below: to know, that is to love, and to serve the Lord; and to practise the virtues of charity and patience, particularly during the trials that life brings us, persevering always in the certainty of eternal goods. (17 August 1960)

69 One of the more beautiful and delicate flowers of our holy Religion is that we are able to speak on intimate terms, tenderly and respectfully, with the Mother of Jesus, who Jesus himself consecrated Mother of all believers. (11 February 1958)

70 This thought, which speaks straight to our heart, illuminates the whole of our lives as Christians: Mary, our Mother! (7 September 1960)

71 Whatever we do, wherever we look, we find that there, always, is Mary, Mother of Jesus and our Mother; and our spirit is at once filled with great serenity and joy. (21 May 1961)

72 On this earth we have need of comfort, of protection, and of a mother's help. And directly from her Immaculate Heart, Mary offers us her incomparable and unfailing embrace. (22 August 1962)

73 Mary his Mother, and in the light of the Redemption, the mother of us all. Every Christian's sighs, from the baby's first words to the final gasp of the dying, are all summed up in this invocation: Holy Mary, Mother of God, pray for us. (15 February 1959)

74 The smile of Mary, Mother of Jesus and our mother, fountain of grace, brings serenity to all who are preoccupied and opens the eyes of souls who are oppressed, discouraged, and tired, to visions of goodness, mercy and trust. (30 April 1955)

75 Life unfolds before us. We leave infancy, adolescence, and we call upon our Mother, again and again. Our pleas become more frequent, above all in life's difficult moments, when we are mature and feel the burden of our responsibility. And so it goes on, decade upon decade, for what seems an age, for a time that seems incredibly long but is nonetheless very real: right into extreme old age. (7 September 1960)

76 The Mother of Jesus, who is our mother – Oh! How I love to bring these two titles together – is one of the richest springs on which we can draw, the richest after Jesus, who of her nature is truly light and life. Mary is a most rich fountain of comfort, joy and encouragement for the children of Eve who, through the redeeming acts and will of Christ, have become her children. (28 August 1955)

77 Whoever loves in the Heart of Mary is able to pass on a love that is strong and authentic, since there is no human love that can be compared with that of a mother. (11 August 1960)

78 Mary is a Mother like no other; she is the gold in the fire of the Christian hearth; she calls all to her so that she can hold them close to her heart. Beside her, you will all feel more like the brothers and sisters you are. (11 August 1960)

79 'Hail, Holy Queen, Mother of Mercy': so begins the poem of a humanity thrown into confusion by sin, subject to tears, suffering and death. And yet despite everything this humanity turns to her, 'life, sweetness, and our hope', and calls upon her as it draws its last breath, a breath that is full of a luminous and un-conquered faith. Show us, 'the blessed fruit of your womb, Jesus. O Clement, O Holy, O Sweet Virgin Mary'.

(1 May 1963)

MARY IMMACULATE

He came to her and said,
'Greetings, favoured one!
The Lord is with you.'
(Lk 1:28)

80 When we think of the word 'immaculate', we think of order and beauty. God placed a distinct order in nature, and raised it up to the level of grace, grace that has barely left the hands of the Creator. As such, nature is therefore docile to God's will and his desires. Beauty derives from this God-given order, and is its luminous crown. (7 December 1959)

81 When we think of the word 'immaculate', we think of the splendour of dawn. Preserved immune from the original contamination. (7 December 1959)

82 After the centuries-long night caused by the sin of our first parents, now this morning star rises, clear and pure, translucent and unblemished, and the heavens become rose-coloured with the promise of the imminent day. (7 December 1959)

83 When we think of the word 'immaculate', we think also of the promise of redemption and its flower of the purest white. (7 December 1959)

84 This woman, who was to give the eternal Word of the Father his mortal flesh, could not have been contaminated, not even for an instant, by the shadow of sin. When we speak of Mary as immaculate we mean that in this she is dependent on Jesus, because she has received everything she has through her dependence on the Son.   (7 December 1959)

85 And finally, when we think of the word 'immaculate', we think of the vision of Paradise. That grace, which was given to Mary in a complete and supereminent degree from the very first moment of her earthly life and is given to us also, though obviously in a lesser measure, is only a pledge of eternal happiness: a pledge for that day when the veils of faith that now conceal the vision of God will drop, and we will contemplate the Lord face to face.   (7 December 1959)

86 What poetry is more beautiful, what sound is more pleasing, than the 'Hail Mary' prayed by a child?
(12 April 1961)

87 O Virgin Immaculate, radiant image of innocence and grace, who dispels the darkness of impending night and lifts us up to the brilliance of heaven, look with kindness upon your children and those who are devoted to you, who fly to your embrace. Star of the Morning, ready our thoughts for the coming of the Sun of Justice, brought by you into the world. Door of heaven, raise up our hearts so that they desire Paradise. Mirror of justice, preserve in us the love of divine grace, so that humble and joyful in the fulfilment of our Christian vocation we may enjoy forever the Lord's friendship and your motherly consolation.   (7 December 1959)

HANDMAID OF THE LORD

Then Mary said:
'My soul magnifies the Lord
and my spirit rejoices in God my Saviour,
for he has looked with favour on the lowliness
of his servant.
Surely, from now on all generations will call me blessed.
(Lk 1:46-48)

88 The first human voice heard in the history of the redemption belonged to the Most Holy Virgin: 'Here am I, the servant of the Lord'.   (13 August 1960)

89 On hearing the angelic voice, the light of the Holy Spirit shone on Mary's face, and penetrated deep into her soul and her immaculate breast. There it brought into being the mystery of her virginal motherhood and gave it life. This mystery was and always will be the greatest wonder of all time – the Heavenly Father's wonder of mercy, who sent his only Son for the redemption of humanity.   (29 May 1955)

90 Magnificat! How sweet it is for us to let the words of the canticle that the Virgin Mary sang at the very beginning of her most wonderful motherhood resound in our souls. And with the word 'Magnificat' Mary began a hymn which has sounded through the ages, telling the whole human race of the joy and comfort that had come to it.   (10 May 1963)

91 Mary's life, which was always humble, docile, simple, pure, infused with love, obedient to the word of the Lord, and generous towards her brothers and sisters, is a mirror of virtue for all times, for all places, and for all creatures. (15 August 1954)

92 To become like Mary means loving humility and simplicity. It means purity of behaviour and meekness in our words, our features, and in our hearts. It means love of home and our daily toil. (28 May 1955)

93 Your birth, O Mary, brought joy to the whole universe. But this joy is also coloured by the blood-red of sacrifice: the sacrifice of the blessed Mother of Jesus, who, when she herself said 'Let it be', agreed to participate in the fate of the Son, in the privations of Bethlehem, in the renouncing of the hidden life at Nazareth, and in his agony on Calvary.

(7 December 1959)

QUEEN

A great portent appeared in heaven:
a woman clothed with the sun,
with the moon under her feet,
and on her head a crown of twelve stars.

(Rev 12:1)

94 The Virgin's greatness lies in her most excellent motherhood. The Liturgy and Christian piety sum up this greatness in the title of 'Queen', a title which encapsulates the power of her intercession and points to the fact that our prayers pass through her blessed hands. (19 September 1959)

95 She is Queen because she moves the heart of her Son and sweetly rules all human hearts.

(19 September 1959)

96 Mary too, the great Mother and Queen of all, worked and suffered in this life, but always in silence, in a spirit of sacrifice, in the joyful and generous fulfilment of God's will. And the Lord exalted her. He did great things for her. He crowned her Queen of all the angelic choirs. (31 May 1959)

97 Raised up to an infinite glory, Mary has not become separate from us, she has not forgotten us: she waits for us, and bends over us to hear our supplications. (16 August 1961)

98 Mary! A most wonderful and significant name, one that moves heaven and earth.

(12 September 1959)

99 Yes, yes, for this we ask you, O most sweet Mother of ours, O Queen of the whole world. The world has no need of victory in war, or peoples defeated, but of a restored and more robust health, of a fruitful peace that puts all in better spirits. The world needs this, and for this we cry aloud.   (10 September 1961)

THE PATH TO CHRIST

His mother said to the servants:
'Do whatever he tells you.'

(Jn 2:5)

100 Devotion to Mary leads us infallibly to our Lord Jesus Christ. And so, any consecration to Mary means also a fervent, binding, and generous consecration to the Divine Saviour, to his law and to his Church.

(19 September 1959)

101 Who loves Jesus, loves also his Mother, and who is dear to such a Mother stands out for their faithfulness to Jesus. (29 August 1961)

102 Jesus can never be separated from his Mother: all the lights that we have been given, all the individual instances of sacred science and zeal in the apostolate, always, always show us Jesus and his Mother together, they never separate Mary from her Divine Son.

(20 November 1962)

103 Mary is with us, she is among us: she protects us, helps us; she leads us by the path that is safe.

(20 November 1962)

104 All leads us to Mary. She is, first of all, the door of heaven; she is also, in all truth, the way through which we can attain an outpouring of grace and the gift of extraordinary graces. (9 September 1962)

105 It becomes clearer every day that the path all must take if they wish to return to God is the path that lies under Mary's protection. She it is we can rely on most; on her is our security based, she is the reason for our hope. (20 August 1959)

THE ROSARY OF MARY

But Mary
treasured all these words
and pondered them in her heart.
(Lk 2:19)

106 The Rosary is a simple way of praying, inviting us always to an inner peace, to abandonment to God, to trust, and then to the certainty that we will obtain the graces that we need.   (13 October 1960)

107 Mary's Rosary: heart and eyes raised in contemplation, as in so many pictures, the contemplation of the central episodes in the life and mission of Jesus and Mary.   (2 October 1955)

108 *Causes of joy.* The angel's annunciation; the canticle on the hill country around Hebron to the blessed among women, started by Mary herself, exalting the wonders that were worked in her; the canticle of the angels proclaiming glory and peace around the crib at Bethlehem; the joyful acclamation of the aged Simeon as he welcomed the Mother of God and the Son of the promise into the Temple; and finally, the firm and gentle voice of this great old man, giving witness to the heavenly Father's will and glory on the threshold of the Temple. So many causes of unutterable joy!   (2 October 1955)

109 *Causes of suffering.* The agony of Jesus; the pains his body endured; the intense pain he suffered when his head was crowned with thorns; his trembling footsteps as he ascended Calvary; and the closing episode of his death in a last outpouring of divine love towards his Mother and the new son he gave her: these separate incidents together form a single image which encapsulates the events and sufferings found in every human life. Is it not thus? (2 October 1955)

110 *Causes of exultation and of triumph.* Jesus alone is truly triumphant. Through his resurrection he triumphed over death; his Father clothed him in glory, raising him in his human nature to enjoy the eternal splendours of divinity; in his Church through the diffusion of the Holy Spirit; the triumph of his Mother through her assumption, glorious coronation, and her proclamation as Queen by all the angels and saints; in the continuation of her glorious motherhood which is now poured out over all the children of the Church who have become, with Christ or through his words, her own children and are now under her protection and recipients of her most wonderful mercy. (2 October 1955)

111 May the Holy Rosary prayed in family bring peace to your homes. Let your children go to Mary to preserve their innocence and their openness. May the young be moved by Mary to do good and to guard their purity with care. May those who suffer receive from her consolation; those who govern, wisdom and prudence. (13 December 1959)

112 Brothers and Sisters: behold the rosary. Behold the Bible of the poor. (2 October 1955)

The Church

MOTHER AND MISTRESS

And I saw the holy city, the new Jerusalem,
coming down out of heaven from God,
prepared as a bride adorned for her husband.
(Rev 21:2)

113 Mother and Mistress of all peoples, the universal Church was instituted by Jesus Christ so that all down through the ages, coming to her and being embraced by her, might find the fullness of the highest life and the guarantee of salvation. (15 May 1961)

114 The Church is virgin, yes, certainly, on account of the purity of her holiness; mother on account of her abundant spiritual fruitfulness; but first of all and always, a spouse of love and of blood. She is intimately united and conformed to Jesus as her head, one with him in heart, will, soul, and intention: she did everything for everyone in order to bring all to the knowledge and love of Jesus, forming with him the perfect mystical body. (1 June 1956)

115 The Catholic Church is not a museum filled with ancient things. She is the ancient village fountain which gives water to today's generations just as she gave it to generations past. (13 November 1960)

116 The voice of the Church is like a mother's voice: it may sound at times monotonous, but it is filled with tenderness and strength, which calls us away from evil and saves us. (15 August 1962)

117 Remember the teachings of the apostolic magisterium, which is always alive and always relevant; like an ancient fountain sitting in a town square it continues to pour forth the purest and freshest of water, restoring, saving and enlightening souls.

(23 February 1955)

118 As the heavenly Father invites you to come to his Son, who made himself our brother, so the Church repeating the holy gesture of Mary, holds out Jesus to you through the priestly ministry.

(25 December 1961)

119 For the world of today the Spouse of Christ prefers to use the medicine of mercy rather than that of severity. (25 December 1961)

120 To old people the Church offers the surest protection. Jesus' light is not weakened by old age; the force that powers us to believe in him, to abandon ourselves trustingly to his promises that never fail and to his safekeeping which is sure, is always alive.

(23 July 1960)

121 The Church of Christ, and with her all those who share the impulse to extend charity to every person, is always present wherever the destiny of peoples is being shaped, wherever people work and suffer. She was not born yesterday. Through the centuries she has lived and fought not with the arms of violence, but with those of charity, of prayer, and of sacrifice: arms that have no equal and cannot be bettered, since they are the arms of her Divine Founder, who in the most solemn hour of his life said to his own, 'But take courage, I have overcome the world!' (Jn 16:33).

(8 May 1960)

122 The Catholic Church has never wished to subject humanity to the harsh law of suffering and death. (11 June 1960)

123 The Church applauds the growing dominion of humankind over the powers of nature. She rejoices in every progress, present and future, which allows humankind to appreciate the infinite grandeur of the Creator more deeply and to render him, with growing admiration and humility, the homage of adoration and thanks that is his due. (24 December 1962)

124 When the light of Christ brings new life to the temporal order, it also reveals each person to themselves, that is, it leads them to discover in themselves their own being, their own divinity, their own end.
(25 December 1961)

LIVING COMMUNITY

We declare to you what we have seen and heard
so that you also may have fellowship with us;
and truly our fellowship is with the Father
and with his Son Jesus Christ.

(1 Jn 1:3)

125 Each person knows, and must know, that they have a place in the Church and it is their job to make sure that they do honour to it.   (7 March 1962)

126 The witness given by individuals needs to be confirmed and extended through the witness given by the whole Christian community, as happened in the early days of the Church, when in a close-knit and persevering union all the faithful 'devoted themselves to the apostles' teaching and fellowship, to the breaking of bread and the prayers' (Acts 2:42) and to the exercise of the most generous charity, which proved to be a cause of profound satisfaction and mutual edification. These early believers, in fact, 'praised God and enjoyed the goodwill of all the people. And day by day the Lord added to their number those who were being saved' (Acts 2:47).   (28 November 1959)

127 We can already find in the Gospel, in a concise form, the outline of the Church's history: a history of faith.   (19 September 1959)

128 The Church lives, just as her Divine Founder lives! The Church moves forward bearing the virtue of life itself, just as Jesus, after he had submitted to the debt owed by mortal nature, passed victoriously beyond the stone barrier that his enemies had placed to seal the entrance to the tomb!　　　(28 March 1959)

129 The grass, the flowers, be they splendid or modest; the shrubs, the plants, the trees that have already reached maturity; all represent perfectly the various ages of those who have been called by grace to belong to the family of Christ.　　(12 August 1961)

130 The simplicity of the tiny David, who stood defiant before the giant, represents in a very real way the catholic, universal, holy, and blessed Church.

(24 June 1961)

131 Those who have a good share of life's experience should take courage from way the young Church built itself up.　　　(4 November 1959)

132 Virginity and chastity are a glory and an incomparable strength of the Catholic Church.

(30 August 1961)

133 Christianity is essentially about love, since God is love.　　　(17 June 1962)

134 The Church will show that she is the Church by being what she always has been: one who is always alive and always young, who feels the rhythm of the time, who clothes herself in fresh splendour in each new century, who shines with new lights, makes fresh conquests, while remaining faithful to what she is, faithful to the divine image imprinted on her face by her Spouse who loves and protects her, Jesus Christ.

(25 December 1961)

135 As Christians we reach out to all people, all homes, and every person. (9 October 1961)

136 The entire mission of Jesus, which he confided to his Church, is, in fact, summed up in the mysterious words: 'I came to bring fire upon the earth' (Lk 12:49). (20 October 1960)

137 Does anyone dare to say that the Church is dying? No. She is and always will be indestructible. While there is life upon this earth, there will be the Holy, Catholic, and Apostolic Church. (24 May 1961)

138 Throughout the centuries, while all the kingdoms of the earth change and all things human demonstrate their fallen nature, the barque of Peter continues her voyage. (24 May 1961)

139 In spite of adversity, which she has experienced in every period of history, the Church continues to fulfil with trust and boldness the precept of her Divine Founder: to teach, to forgive, to restore to health, and to pass on the supernatural life of grace, in preparation for the eternal enjoyment of glory. (4 November 1959)

140 The blessed Lord keeps his Church close to him and inspires her, suggesting to her actions she might take, tempering any fervour that might seethe within her, and giving her a sense of the due proportion of things. (7 March 1962)

BODY OF CHRIST

The cup of blessing that we bless,
is a communion with the blood of Christ.
The bread that we break,
is a communion in the body of Christ.
Because there is one bread,
we who are many are one body,
for we all partake
of the one bread.

(1 Cor 10:16-17)

141 No. Christ the Son of God and Our Saviour has not left the world he redeemed. The Church which he founded, one, holy, catholic, and apostolic remains his mystical body forever. He is the head of this body. We as believers belong to this body, and we take our bearings from it. (14 November 1960)

142 The Church, from its beginnings right up to our own days has never known a time of peace. And yet it has always kept the same undiminished vigour and strength because it was founded by Jesus Christ on the firmest of rocks. (14 December 1959)

143 If we remain united to this rock, we will never know defeat nor error, but will participate in its own strength, which comes from on high. (11 May 1961)

144 Whoever stands with the Church finds their feet on solid ground, they are sure in their every work and know that all they do finds a response, a resonance in heaven. (10 November 1953)

145 The Church, even though she may seem to be flooded with troubles and anxieties, is always glorious, since Christ is present within her.

(24 September 1959)

146 In the holy Church of Jesus, we learn how to rejoice with those who rejoice and weep with those who weep; and in the rejoicing and the weeping we taste the sweetness and consolation of true brotherhood and sisterhood. (1 April 1956)

147 You must never cease to feel yourselves to be living members of this Church which is our mother, and so, through the witness that each one of you gives she will appear to be in our time what she really is, and what her founder, Jesus, wished her to be: one, holy, catholic. (11 May 1961)

148 Faithful Christians, who are members of a living organism, cannot remain closed inside themselves believing that they have exhausted their duty by providing for their own spiritual needs. Each one has their own contribution to the growth and expansion of God's kingdom on the earth.

(28 November 1959)

149 The embrace of peace which the children of the same heavenly Father, the equal co-heirs to the same kingdom of glory, will give each other will mark the celebration of the triumph of Christ's mystical body.

(11 November 1961)

WORD OF GOD

And so shall my word,
that goes out from my mouth,
never return to me empty,
without having accomplished my purpose
and having succeeded in the thing for which I sent it.

(Isa 55:11)

150 Christian Revelation contains the treasures of the Word of God that pours light and goodness into our souls. (15 February 1961)

151 The Word of God is able to move any person, regardless of their age and condition, thanks to the power that it carries deep within itself.

(13 November 1961)

152 Meditate on the individual psalms in order to discover the secret beauty within them and to gain a sure *sense of God* and a *sense of the Church*. Rest in them. Raise yourselves from the psalms to the contemplation of heavenly things, and from these turn to a just and exact appreciation of earthly things, of culture and of history, and of daily events.

(28 January 1960)

153 The words of Christ have been sown in every century. Each word is a seed that promises a boundless harvest. The doctrine never changes and never loses the power to save every one of us. (5 March 1961)

154 In the confusion and muddle created by so many human words, the Gospel alone provides a voice that enlightens, attracts, comforts us, and quenches our thirst. (13 February 1961)

155 Behold the Gospel: therein is contained the entire essence of the Church's life.
(19 September 1959)

156 That which is sublime in the Gospel is not a torrent that sends its echoes reverberating throughout the mountains from which it comes crashing down, rather it is a tranquil river whose waters are always abundant and whose majesty is ever wonderful; it is not the sudden flash of illumination which precedes the storm, but the gradual and calm diffusion of a serene light that spreads out at its own pace until it has filled the earth and the heavens.
(15 February 1956)

157 The Gospel and peace: two things that always go together. (25 April 1961)

158 The solution to our problems does not lie in hatred, nor does the secret of the world's renewal lie in the triumph of anti-Christian ideologies, but rather in the freely-given, consistent, and firm living of the Gospel, even where this calls for personal sacrifice.
(1 May 1959)

159 There is no possibility that Marxism and the Gospel could ever be in agreement. And we cannot sacrifice the Gospel to Marxism. (9 June 1956)

160 It is the holy Gospel that really counts, the radiant sun of heavenly doctrine that has illuminated the course of two thousand years of civilisation. This alone can guide humanity towards its centuries-old and eternal destiny, ever alive and ever young with Jesus Christ, the Divine Master of every century, and the splendour of truth, grace, and glory.

(10 August 1959)

161 Serve the word of God well, make its beauty and newness resound everywhere, without impoverishing or changing it, but making it full of life and attractive. (18 October 1959)

161 A true member of the faithful loves the Gospel, savours its immense spiritual treasures, identifies with it and makes sure that their life conforms to each page within it, to every one of its teachings that the Saviour of the World offers for the salvation of all.

(5 November 1960)

EUCHARIST

*Those who eat my flesh
and drink my blood have eternal life,
and I will raise them up on the last day;
for my flesh is true food
and my blood is true drink.*

(Jn 6:54-55)

163 The earth lives, moves, and has its very existence in the sacrifice of the Mass.　　(21 November 1961)

164 Private devotions are very worthy, and they have their value; but nothing, in the estimation of the Christian, must be placed above the holy sacrifice of the Mass.　　(1 January 1961)

165 You will always find the strength to maintain your resolve when you draw close to the holy altar where, for greatest possible good of our souls, the memorial of Christ's passion is enacted.

(1 January 1961)

166 The Mass is the most adorable sacrifice in which God himself is at once victim, priest and the divine Majesty to whom the sacrifice is offered: what happens is not a mere shadow of Christ's sacrifice on the cross, but the very sacrifice itself, renewed and repeated in an unceasing and bloodless mystery.

(21 September 1958)

167 During the holy sacrifice of the Mass, the Blood of Jesus Christ comes down upon us and covers us, our lives, and our souls. This blood makes us holy, redeems us, and inebriates us.   (10 September 1961)

168 The holy Mass brings the human person into the closest possible relationship with the Lord, with him who has created and redeemed us.

(28 February 1960)

169 The Sacrament of the Eucharist, a living and marvellous image of the unity of the Church, communicates to us the Author of supernatural grace himself so that through this communication we might receive that spirit of charity which enables us to live not our own life but that of Christ, and to love the Redeemer in all those who belong to his body.

(13 August 1963)

170 In the obedience of the Mass we find a summary of perfection: to live the Mass is the most perfect way to be a Christian.   (22 September 1961)

171 The Eucharist, infusing the new energy of supernatural love into the human heart, strengthens, channels, and purifies human affections, making them more lasting and authentic. When the human person carries God in their heart, they are in complete harmony with themselves.   (15 February 1959)

172 Through the Sacrament of the Eucharist the faithful receive the virtues which shine so brilliantly in the Divine Saviour, who is full of grace and truth and in whose fullness we have all partaken.   (4 July 1961)

173 In the Eucharist the people of God, enlightened by the proclamation of the faith and nourished by the body of Christ, find their life, growth, and, if there is need, the restoration of the unity which should exist between them. (1 August 1959)

174 The Eucharist is by its very nature a sacrament of unity and of peace. All those who glory in the name of Christian, if they receive this sacrament with a spirit of devotion and holiness, become intimately united with God and with each other in a close bond, a bond that creates of them a society, an assembly, a body. Nothing should be more alien to those who nourish themselves on this food than hostility, hatred, and envy, all of which destroy the union that exists between brothers and sisters. (2 August 1959)

175 In the intimate contact with Jesus, life-giving Word and nourishing Food, your faith is strengthened, your hope is raised up to delightful certainty, and your charity grows more ardent. (1 August 1962)

176 The Eucharist is not concerned solely with the good of the individual communicant, but, as the Angelic Doctor, St Thomas Aquinas, says, with the common spiritual good of the entire Church which is substantially present during the celebration.
(13 September 1959)

177 In the Divine Sacrament the Lord comes among us in silence in order to listen to every one of us.
(25 March 1962)

THE JOURNEY OF THE LITURGY

O sing to the Lord a new song;
sing to the Lord, all the earth.
Sing to the Lord, bless his name;
tell of his salvation from day to day.
(Ps 96:1-2)

Christmas

178 This is Christmas. The Son of God become man draws near to us, not in power, not in terror, but in divine and human goodness. (25 December 1956)

179 The silence of that night, and our contemplation of that scene of peace, are most eloquent. Let us turn to Bethlehem with a pure gaze, and with an open heart. (22 December 1960)

180 At Bethlehem history received a new direction: that the civilisation of each people might spread ever wider; but the responsibility for this new direction has been entrusted to each one of us.
(25 December 1962)

181 Christmas brings great joy to our houses, even in those places where there is weeping, where sorrow and anxiety dwell. (19 December 1962)

182 Around Jesus' crib his angels sang songs of peace. And those who believed the heavenly message and gave honour to the Lord, received glory and rejoiced. So it was yesterday, and so it will be in all ages. (25 December 1962)

183 All that we have comes from that baby, the baby who is given to each one of us by his Mother, and offered to the entire world. (19 December 1962)

184 Let Christmas mark, as it should, the high tide of our peaceful and religious fervour. Let there be an outpouring of charity towards our brothers and sisters who are in need and who are sick, and let us be united with them. The little ones and those who suffer, each and every one of them regardless of who or what they are. (23 December 1958)

185 Let us recognise him with joy. It gives great delight to see the shining eyes of the children gathered round the crib. Even greater is the tenderness when we ourselves return to the crib, in simplicity and humility, little with them and like them! (15 December 1954)

Epiphany

186 The gold that the magi offer represents living faith; the incense, prayer; the myrrh, the sweetness which can never be found unalloyed with afflictions and bitterness. (6 January 1959)

Lent

187 The season of Lent offers to our spirit thoughts and sentiments which are of the highest importance, and which concern the reality of the passage from this earthly existence to the heavenly one. Such matters do not disturb the Christian soul, but lend it support and give it a sense of real security. (1 March 1963)

188 Through the institution of Lent, the Church desired to lead her children not to simple, exterior practices, but rather to the serious task of love and generosity for the good of one's brothers and sisters, in the light of the ancient teaching of the prophets.

(27 February 1963)

189 We must all use this time of Lent to put a holy freshness into our hearts, our works, into what we say; and this freshness will lead us to the true joy that Christ brought into the world and which he continually renews in the triumph of his Passover.

(23 February 1955)

Holy Week

190 During the Liturgy in Holy Week Jesus passes over the earth and draws near to the dwellings of humankind. The innocent little children at once escorted him, the first to do so, as he entered on the back of a humble donkey. They waved fresh olive branches around him and sang, 'Hosanna, hosanna'; the adults and the young people spread their cloaks on the ground before him, they too greeted him with the ancient canticle. (10 April 1960)

191 The passion of Christ, symbolised by the Cross, is for us sacrament and example. (23 September 1959)

192 The voices of humankind and those of the bells are both stilled on this day of great recollection, Holy Saturday. The melancholy liturgical response inviting the faithful to fix their eyes on the sepulchre of the Saviour of the world seems to float on air. Our Shepherd, the fount of living water, has departed, and he dies as the sun is covered over.   (16 April 1960)

Easter

193 Death and life contest with each other in a tremendous duel. The master of life triumphs over death: and his victory is the victory of his Church throughout the centuries.   (23 March 1959)

194 'Christ, our Passover, has been sacrificed' (1 Cor 5:7). Sacrifice is the only way to attain that life, glory, and true success in which lies the true good of each and every person.   (1 April 1963)

195 Easter speaks to us of everlasting youth: it represents the absolute victory of Christ. We will all participate in this triumph.   (18 April 1962)

196 The source of this joy is to be found in the risen Christ, who frees humanity from the slavery of sin, and invites us to become a new creature with him and await the blessedness of eternity.
     (28 March 1959)

197 Easter is for us all a mystery of death and of life: for this reason, according to the express precept of the Church, to which I recall your attention in a fatherly way, each member of the faithful is invited at this time to purify their conscience through the Sacrament of Penance, bathing it in the blood of Jesus; likewise is each member called to draw near to the Eucharistic banquet with greater faith, so that they can nourish themselves on the life-giving flesh of the immaculate Lamb. So the mystery of Easter concerns the death and resurrection of each believer.

(28 March 1959)

Pentecost

198 Pentecost is nothing other than a poem to grace, light, and charity. (4 October 1962)

The human person

IMAGE OF GOD

Then God said,
'Let us make humankind in our image,
according to our likeness;
and let them have dominion over the fish of the sea,
and over the birds of the air,
and over the cattle,
and over all the wild animals of the earth,
and over every creeping thing that creeps upon the earth.'
(Gen 1:26)

199 The human person stands at the very apex of creation, reflecting the light from God's face and destined, as the masterpiece of this same creation, to give voice and meaning to all the creatures.
(28 November 1960)

200 The very concept of the human person contains the highest notions of strength and goodness.
(16 August 1959)

201 Created in the image and likeness of God and redeemed by the precious blood of Christ, the human person must be at the very centre of our concern.
(4 January 1963)

202 Women no less than men are necessary for the progress of society, especially in all those areas that require tact, sensitivity, and maternal intuition.
(6 November 1961)

203 The people of the age in which we live, thinking themselves to be sufficient in everything, fall all too easily in the forgetfulness of divine laws; and so, deprived of the spiritual sun, they risk entombment in an ice-age winter. (4 April 1959)

204 Even today the world has great need of maternal sensitivity to somehow dispel the atmosphere of violence and coarseness in which we sometimes find people struggling against each other.

(6 September 1961)

205 The vocation to motherhood belongs so naturally to women, and fits so well on them, that it is present and alive even when there is no actual physical motherhood. (6 September 1961)

206 Every single person is on a journey towards Christ; some, many, do so unknowingly; and the star illuminates their steps. (9 August 1961)

207 Keep far away, O Lord, every harm that might come to your children from the journey's difficulty, the body's weariness, or a rash haste… And as you gave, O Lord, the Archangel Raphael to the son of Tobias to be his companion on the way, free your children from every danger of soul and body, so that they may walk uprightly in your presence through the paths of the world and might be found worthy to stand before the doors of eternal salvation. Through Christ Our Lord. Amen. Amen. (9 August 1961)

BODY AND SPIRIT

Do you not know that your
body is a temple of the Holy Spirit within you,
which you have from God,
and that you are not your own?
For you were bought with a price;
therefore glorify God in your body.

(1 Cor 6:19-20)

208 We are more than just material beings, but souls, flame that rises up to heaven.   (30 May 1962)

209 The body, which we use and whose suppleness and harmonious construction allows us to catch a glimpse of the beauty and omnipotence of the Creator, is only an instrument that we should render docile and open to the powerful influence of the soul.

(26 April 1959)

210 There are many reasons to bless and thank the Lord, since in this series of contests and competitions, all of which have praiseworthy aims, we can see the union of two realities that often seem to end up divorced from one another: heaven and earth, spirit and matter.   (27 August 1960)

211 The great value of sport lies in its particular effectiveness as an aid to the process of interior growth. This inner growth is attained through exterior discipline and must be the object of the persevering and constant training to which you subject your body.

(26 April 1959)

212 The gifts and good qualities that we can develop through sporting competitions are many and of great value: the body benefits from improved health, vigour, agility, and grace; the soul from perseverance, strength, and the ability to exercise self-restraint.

(24 August 1960)

213 Our recreation must be imbued with the Gospel spirit: fairness, a sense of brotherhood, courteousness, and goodness towards all.   (28 January 1957)

214 Any rules for a healthy upbringing within the family and for the formation of young people must be careful to ensure that competitive sport is not focused entirely on the body, as the supreme good of the human person, and that passion for sport does not prevent the proper fulfilment of one's duties. (24 August 1960)

215 You must know how to bring the same diligence to spiritual combat and to the struggle for the eternal crown as you bring to competitive sport. You must belong to those who are striving to take possession of the Kingdom of Heaven, dedicated to rendering your bodies docile to the motions of the Spirit and your souls obedient to the inspirations of grace.

(25 September 1960)

216 This body, which occupies so much of our thought and preoccupies us with its maintenance, healing, and protection from enemies, is liable to be the object of temptations. For this reason we must remember its great dignity: it leaves the waters of baptism purified, and grace penetrates it in holy communion. Let us recall in every moment that we are living tabernacles of the Lord.   (13 March 1960)

TRUTH

But those who do what is true come to the light,
so that it may be clearly seen
that their deeds have been done in God.

(Jn 3:21)

217 God is the spring, the source, of truth, and God is all truth; and Jesus, the Word of God, spoke clearly: 'I am the truth' (Jn 14:6). This kind of declaration would be worthy of a mad person, were it not to have come from the lips of God made man.

(24 November 1940)

218 Truth is the very light of God, the Creator and supreme Legislator who orders the universe. It is a reflection of his divine essence.   (21 January 1958)

219 The truth is light, and we must immerse our entire persons in it, for it helps shape all our actions.

(22 December 1960)

220 It is wrong to think of our lives as Christians as dedication to a collection of odd ideas and values from the past.   (7 November 1962)

221 Life's great quest lies without doubt in the following: the search for the truth, respect for the truth, and the defence of truth.   (21 January 1958)

222 We must proclaim the truth, place ourselves at its service in every moment: for the truth is holy.

(30 August 1959)

223 Be living witnesses to the truth: this way you will never cease to enjoy a simple and profound joy of heart. (2 June 1962)

224 The announcement and defence of the truth can sometimes cost sacrifice and tears: but it is the truth that liberates us, and in it Christ shines forth. (30 January 1955)

225 The truth is something sacred, something that should never be betrayed. (6 November 1958)

226 Always, always the truth; but when we speak the truth, or write it, we must do so with respect and courtesy. We must speak it to others as we would like to hear it spoken to ourselves, and in a manner not to offend the holy reasons of divine and human laws, of innocence, of justice, and of peace. (29 January 1956)

227 It is not only those who deliberately distort the truth who are guilty, but those also who, fearing to appear lacking or not completely up to date, betray it through the ambiguity of their attitudes. (22 December 1960)

228 This is the right road: the truth. Yes. Always and with all those we meet. But there is more than one way of speaking it. (30 January 1955)

229 All the evils which poison men and nations and trouble so many hearts, have a single cause and a single source: ignorance of the truth – and at times even more than ignorance, a contempt for truth and a reckless rejection of it. (29 June 1959)

230 Putting everything and everyone to shame, the truth of the Lord endures forever, blazing before our eyes and calling out to be received in our hearts.

(22 December 1960)

231 If we wish our own life and that of our neighbour to be worthy of the highest end to which it is called, we must always keep ourselves firmly and without blemish in the exercise of the truth.

232 We must speak the truth to all, we must spread it abroad with courtesy and charity, so that it may attract and fascinate. (1 October 1961)

233 In the strength of the truth go to all: wherever there is intelligence to enlighten, wills to strengthen, and energies to channel for the good; wherever there are tears to wipe, uncertainties to overcome, and solitude where light and life are wanting. (1 May 1959)

FREEDOM

For you were called to freedom, brothers and sisters;
only do not use your freedom
as an opportunity for self-indulgence,
but through love become slaves
to one another.

(Gal 5:13)

234 True freedom is a gift of the Lord, and it can flower and prosper only where his Spirit blows. Where there is the Spirit of the Lord there is freedom, as St Paul admonished. (19 May 1959)

235 To every soul who comes into this life the Lord has given a gold coin: freedom of choice. We should put this gift to good use; with it every one of God's creatures holds their salvation or perdition in their own hands. (23 February 1955)

236 The Lord created heaven and earth: the sun to give light to the day, and the moon for the night. Even after the first sin, followed by the promise of redemption and grace, he left humankind with the freedom of choice, the uncompromised ability to choose between light and darkness, between good and evil. (15 April 1956)

237 Both the negation of God and the direct or indirect oppression of one's neighbour or the diminishing of their inalienable rights due to them as free persons, and persons possessed of a Christian vocation, show equal scorn for the light of heaven. (28 June 1962)

238 If God is ignored, freedom becomes like a word written on the waters of the sea.

Without his help no building can be constructed to last, neither will the vigilance of those who watch over a city be sufficient for its defence.

(19 May 1959)

239 The exercise of our freedom becomes, in the light and the grace of Christ, a life of love and sacrifice and love lived in devotion and rejoicing, while we spend our earthly life as a preparation for the heavenly life that awaits us on the other shore.   (24 June 1956)

240 When we are speaking of sad times or happy times as if either were absolute, our observations bear no real resemblance to things as they actually are. Each age has its miseries and its splendours. The ugliness, or the beauty, of an age is determined by the ignorance, the malice, or the goodness of the people of the time.

(15 April 1956)

241 Your glory lies in your freedom, yes, but the freedom of God's children.   (19 May 1959)

PURITY

Blessed are the pure in heart,
for they will see God.
(Mt 5:8)

242 Before all things, purity of heart; and in the keeping of an unceasing vigilance and constant attention this purity gives order and transparency to our whole life, and to our every word and every act.
(22 November 1959)

243 Devotion to purity is the most precious honour and treasure of the Christian family: it is a sure pledge of every earthly and heavenly blessing. (8 June 1962)

244 This virtue is the charm of every Christian family, and in that soil it flourishes as in its natural environment, exercising an irresistible fascination over souls. Blanketing over the filth that unfortunately covers the greater part of this poor world which lies under the dominion of the evil one, purity draws respect from those whose lives are far from pure, even those who have at times spoken derisively of it.
(22 November 1959)

245 The serene atmosphere created by purity of heart is required by every serious vocation, it is the soil in which all the other good dispositions can grow and mature. (22 November 1959)

246 Of course, it cannot be considered as the first of virtues in the sense that, should anyone be lacking in love for God or neighbour, then purity becomes a cold exercise in natural perfection: but it is the very breath of God's love and the indispensable condition for a disinterested service of one's neighbour.

(22 November 1959)

247 Purity it is that prepares us for the incomparable joys of our conversations at the foot of the Tabernacle; it nourishes the most ardent thoughts of charity and of our apostolic work, which inspires in us an unbroken serenity and which neither fail in adversity nor plunge into excess in times of joy.   (22 November 1959)

248 When I am in danger of sinning against holy purity, then more urgently than ever will I appeal to God, to my Guardian Angel and to Mary, with my familiar invocation: 'Mary Immaculate, help me.'

(*JS*, 8 December 1897)

249 We must remain faithful to Christ, and be prepared, if necessary, to shed our blood in order to maintain purity of body and soul.

(26 November 1961)

STRENGTH

I will trust, and will not be afraid,
for the Lord God is my strength and my song;
he has become my salvation.

(Is 12:2)

250 Strength is not boldness; it is not haste; it is not the overpowering of others in a pride-filled affirmation of self; neither is it the exclusive domain of the body, to the detriment of the strength of intelligence and of heart, of kindness and of goodness.

(20 May 1960)

251 You can always be masters of yourselves, directing your intellect, heart, and tongue towards the good: three things which have a great value in anyone who wishes to gain some degree of self-possession and composure in their lives, especially precious in times of confusion and bewilderment such as we are living in now. (7 March 1962)

252 Strength ensures that our intellect, will, and sensitivity remain in perfect balance. (29 January 1960)

253 A soul which is large and strong will never fall prey to sadness, not even in the hour of the most severe tribulation. (29 January 1960)

254 Perfect virginity and a strength which can withstand anything reveal their presence in a joyfulness of spirit, word, and deed, and a complete detachment from every 'right' that our egos presume to possess.

(29 January 1960)

255 Strength keeps us humble because it is well aware of its own limits and inadequacies; it produces meekness within us, it leads us to be obedient, and it is a sure school for strong souls. Because of it we yield, in order to serve better; we are masters of ourselves, so that we can attract souls to God through gentleness; we have overcome ourselves, so that Christ's power may dwell in us. (29 January 1960)

256 Stand firm in the Lord so that you may keep that steadiness and resolution which is the mark of the strong and courageous. (24 July 1960)

257 What the Church wants is people who are firm and steadfast, well formed in mind and heart. Fortunately that time is past when, knowing nothing of the strength and vigour of the Church, many saw her children as weak and somewhat lacking, almost entirely without a backbone. Rather, being a member of the Church demands an adamantine temperament in both character and will, a continual struggle against the passions and egoism, and the overcoming of oneself through the Lord's help. (22 November 1959)

258 Let us stand firm in the Lord that we might know him, love him, and serve him; we are nourished through grace with his own life; and we are fed on his precious Body, a pledge of eternal life and of future glory. (24 July 1960)

PERFECTION

Be perfect, therefore,
as your heavenly Father is perfect.
(Mt 5:48)

259 Perfection in this life consists in the absolute renunciation of our own point of view and in striving to do all that God wishes us to, and that alone.
(25 November 1962)

260 Let us have a living and firm faith that nothing spiritual is able to halt: our faith is joyful, it takes the greatest delight in the light of God.
(16 September 1959)

261 The human heart, like the intellect, is always thirsting to touch the absolute and become one with it.
(5 October 1962)

262 Truly called wise is the person who knows how to watch, to observe, and study, so that all the needs to be done is accomplished to perfection, and completed as it should be.
(18 August 1962)

263 God is not pleased with things done by halves, or grudgingly.
(*JS*, 21 September 1898)

264 Everyone has a duty to examine their past history, to reflect on their own ever-present inadequacies, and to find a remedy. Let us all strive to give fresh impetus to our spiritual lives, to pray better, and to practise much more convincingly the virtues that we stand in great need of, patience, generosity, and joyful acceptance of sacrifice.
(4 January 1962)

265 It is essential that we know how to have a properly balanced relationship with ourselves and with our neighbour. (18 July 1962)

266 Not great and extraordinary achievements, but great perfection in everyday matters.

(*JS*, 8 August 1898)

267 Rather than thinking about the past, we feel that we have to do all we can to ensure a better and a more secure future. (25 November 1962)

268 Each one of us should aim at the full conquest of our own inner life, of that true supernatural beauty which is within. The gifts of each individual shine out, their lights and those of their neighbours spreading out ever further into the distance, rejoicing in each other, and making the great family of believers ever more beautiful. (7 December 1959)

269 Among all the peaks which as Christians and human beings we can ascend, the very highest is to be sought here: direct contact with Jesus through his body and blood. (1 June 1956)

270 The Lord has put us upon this earth so that we might exercise ourselves in all that renders our lives perfect, keeping constantly in mind that we must never lose that light and splendour that comes from above.

(27 August 1960)

271 Let us move forward at every moment with greater generosity, knowing that we do not walk in the dark, but in the light; our way is lit not by the lamps of this world which deceive, but by the perfect splendours of Christ. (15 June 1959)

God
and the
human person

CHILDREN OF GOD

See what love the Father has given us,
that we should be called children of God;
and that is what we are.
The reason the world does not know us
is that it did not know him.

(1 Jn 3:1)

272 No human being could ever fully appreciate what it means to live the gift – the joyful, ardent, committed and victorious gift – of life in God, with the Holy Spirit, in his Church, and with his Gospel.

(3 April 19593)

273 God's own clarity and purity fills the human person with great dignity and strength, marking them with the splendour of the Heavenly Father.

(19 June 1961)

274 Be strong and generous, and do not forget the greatness that is yours as a Christian and child of God. Only then will you feel the guiding hand of your heavenly Father's providence.   (23 April 1961)

275 Without God, there can be nothing but unhappiness and restlessness.   (7 January 1962)

276 We must not encourage those passions, those weaknesses, or those attitudes of carelessness that lead us to break off relations with the Creator, nor should we allow them to gain a foothold. All that is bad, all that is contrary to the supreme law, is not worthy of a child of God.   (27 August 1960)

277 God created people as friends, not enemies.

(26 June 1959)

278 I will not forget that I am never alone, even when I am by myself: God, Mary and my Guardian Angel can see me. (*JS*, 8 December 1897)

FAITH

For whatever is born of God conquers the world.
And this is the victory that conquers the world,
our faith.

(1 Jn 5:4)

279 The most lofty poem of Christian life derives its force above all from faith: faith which imbues us with a profound peace, and blazes in splendour.

(19 July 1961)

280 Faith is, as it were, the air of Christian life, and who notices and pays any attention to the air we breathe? (*JS*, 18 December 1903)

281 Beware! The faith into which you were born and in which you grew up is not a fable, nor is it an invention. It is centuries old, and was confirmed by Jesus through his teachings on charity, forgiveness, and self-denial. Through these teachings we learn to consecrate ourselves to Christ's own work, which is the truest and highest expression of civilisation.

(3 March 1960)

282 Neither faith alone, nor works alone, but the perfect working together of the two. It is this kind of faith, enlightened, full of conviction, and rich in good works to a greater or lesser extent, by which the stature of the perfect Christian can be measured; by it the perfect Christian can be distinguished from the person who is weak, slothful, unhappy, and almost of no account. (23 November 1955)

283 Every believer knows that they have the supernatural spirit dwelling within them. This Spirit urges us as believers to build on firm rock rather than sandy ground, so that we can defy the raging winds and persevere to eternal life.   (22 September 1962)

284 This is the victory that conquers the world: faith in Christ. This faith is above all a grace from the Lord. As such we must cultivate it, preserving it in our families, letting its most beneficial light penetrate all aspect of our lives. We must be ready to shed our own blood rather than repudiate it or betray it.
(28 August 1955)

285 Discouragement can come only from a lack of faith. Was it not the very same master who said to Simon when he was discouraged: 'Man of little faith, why did you doubt?' (Mt 14:31)   (24 June 1961)

286 Faith is the Christian root from which good fruit must grow: among these fruits Christian humility, the sister of charity, must be conspicuous.
(14 January 1959)

287 Only the Christian view of reality is capable of uncovering the deepest aspects of human nature, and of showing our contemporaries the star we ought to follow.   (1 January 1957)

288 Faith lights up the inner person, it is a living flame. When a flame spreads it often burns and cracks the material which it is burning.   (4 January 1954)

289 The Christian faith has nothing to fear from science, or from the technology which derives from it. On the contrary, the possibilities that science opens up are, in fact, a glorification of the creative goodness of God, who said to us: 'Fill the earth and subdue it' (Gen 1:28).   (30 December 1959)

290 I must take into account everything, however insignificant or even not fully confirmed by facts or sound reasons, in order to nourish my faith, never allowing it to grow stale, and in order to enrich it with a vigorous and whole-hearted determination and also with indescribable tenderness and appealing simplicity.
(*JS*, 18 December 1903)

291 On the wings of faith and of prayer we lift ourselves ever closer to the Lord. Thus we are able to combine the passing of time with supernatural life.
(4 January 1962)

292 Nourish your faith, my dear children: faith in God, just and merciful, without whom our lives would be like a sunless day, like a universe plunged into darkness; faith in the Church which, through God's willing it, guides all people to heaven, with goodness and surety.   (4 April 1959)

HOPE

May the God of hope
fill you with all joy and peace in believing,
so that you may abound in hope
by the power of the Holy Spirit.

(Rom 15:13)

293 Know how to wait, but work while you are waiting. (17 February 1957)

294 We must await the continual help that comes from the Lord with the knowledge that we have fulfilled our duty and with great humility. On him is founded our strength, and on him the certainty that we will continue to follow the good path. (3 June 1959)

295 If evil is a sad reality, today as yesterday, it nevertheless will never be able – as we know well – to overcome good. (17 February 1962)

296 Whatever happens – and nothing fatal can ever happen if we have a firm and profound faith in the Giver of every good – we will remain firm in our hope. (2 September 1961)

297 Let us be strong in faith and, at Jesus' side, we will be able to cross not only the small sea in Galilee, but every sea in the world. The word of Jesus is enough to rescue us and give victory. (22 December 1960)

298 There seems to be a fairly widely diffused belief that the world is currently passing through terrible times. But history records that there have been much worse times in the past: and despite the loud or deceitful voices of the violent we remain certain that the spiritual victory will be won by Christ.   (22 December 1960)

299 We do not fear what the future may hold, since time is in the hands of the Creator of heaven and earth, and the souls that the Son of God has redeemed through his blood are destined for salvation, peace, and eternal glory.   (17 October 1962)

300 Even though we may have to suffer greatly, our hope is founded on Jesus; and when Jesus founded his Church he did not intend to exclude trial and persecution. To him rises the cry of trust and hope: 'Let not those who hope in you be put to confusion… remember your mercies, for they have been of old' (cf Ps 25). To him rises the unceasing prayer that the brothers and sisters who are being persecuted may obtain constancy and firmness, and that their per-secutors, who 'do not know what they do' (Lk 23:24), may receive light, forgiveness, and be converted.

(17 May 1959)

301 The Lord leaves us uncertain about our eternal salvation, but he gives us signs which suffice to calm our souls and make us joyful.

(*JS*, 28 November 1940)

302 The words of the Saviour remain living and certain, always. The final victory will be ours: not a victory won through violence, domination, destruction of peoples, or tempests, but through charity poured out everywhere, and through sweetness.

(7 June 1961)

CHARITY

So we have known and believe
the love that God has for us. God is love,
and those who abide in love abide in God,
and God abides in them.

(1 Jn 4:16)

303 Charity and goodness are the very best fruits of Christianity. (16 August 1959)

304 In life, as you know, it is not the noise you make or the things you see that count, but the love with which you fulfil God's will. (29 July 1959)

305 Always charity! May it go before us and accompany our footsteps, since it is the only way to be sure that God's blessing will be on all our undertakings and all that we do. (19 October 1954)

306 Meekness, and humility of heart are the distinctive traits of Christian charity. (3 March 1957)

307 Faith is indispensable; hope is excellent; but only charity is perfect and irreplaceable. Through faith we obtain the light that we need; hope is a fountain of consolation; charity is the great certainty.

(19 July 1961)

308 The 'fullness of the law' (Rom 13:10), charity, is necessary for the ordered and faithful fulfilment of our daily duties, from the greatest to the least.

(22 November 1959)

309 Among all those things which can be done in the world, and which are great and worthy of praise, charity practised and lived is the only one that endures and shines with the purest light from now to eternity. Charity will never end.

310 Charity is the highest Christian virtue and the one which brings us closest to God. (31 January 1962)

311 Each one of us in the different dwelling places (cf Jn 14:2) to which we are called, can, must, repeat with Peter: Lord you know very well that I love you and believe in you (cf Jn 21:17).   (27 June 1962)

312 Charity goes hand in hand with truth.
(10 November 1959)

313 The rose stands out from all the other flowers. Its colour indicates charity, its perfume recalls the sweetness and the generous toil that we undertake to conform ourselves to the spirit of Christ; and Christ's spirit, as long as we are on this earth, is a spirit of suffering.   (1 June 1962)

314 Charity, desiring to do God's will, is able to do everything: it hopes in all things, it bears all things.
(11 May 1963)

315 Just as the blood, coursing silently through our veins, gives life, colour and strength to the entire body, so charity, a hidden but pulsing and life-giving force, makes all our good works effective and meritorious.
(8 March 1959)

316 Charity is the result and the summit of all the other good dispositions. It must permeate our every act, thought and feeling.   (31 January 1962)

317 While people today grow cold in their charity, you must burn even more brightly with God's love.
(26 September 1959)

318 Charity is the mysterious force that prepares us for the day of the Lord.   (10 August 1962)

THE WILL OF GOD

Father, if you are willing,
remove this cup from me!
Yet let not my will be done
but yours.
(Lk 22:42)

319 If we wish to remain joyful and cheerful, the most important condition is to be at peace with the Lord. (9 January 1963)

320 A most important point: God's will must be fulfilled without pause, even if this sometimes requires sacrifice on our part. (29 October 1960)

321 Before us always the Cross; over us the will of God. (11 November 1962)

322 Take a path that is pleasing to God: this is the greatest and the most noble aim we can have in life, and an inexhaustible source of the purest satisfaction. (24 July 1960)

323 Our true greatness lies in the total and perfect fulfilment of God's will. (*JS*, 6 February 1903)

324 Blessedness is a state of tranquil knowledge, in which we rest in the security of having fulfilled not our own wills, but that of God. (10 March 1956)

325 Let us make continual progress in this most wonderful disposition of the soul: to wish for nothing except that which pleases God and to make it your rule to serve the Church and help your neighbour to salvation through prayer, your daily activities, and the example of virtue. (20 August 1959)

326 Everything becomes meritorious when we walk down the paths of obedience. (11 May 1961)

327 We will never want for crosses. Each one of us must carry their own cross if they wish to transform themselves into the perfect image of Christ. But we are able to bear this sweet burden, with pleasure even, if it is accompanied by the sweetness and peace that comes from the tranquility of a Christian conscience and by living in full conformity to the Lord's will. (4 October 1962)

328 Adore the merciful designs of Divine Providence in a spirit of faith and humility of heart. For this Providence makes the sorrow of today holy, and through this sorrow prepares for the joy of tomorrow; it causes God's grace to fall copiously, fruitfully, on the furrows that had been ploughed by suffering. (28 December 1958)

329 Enjoyment of God's love, the sweet and total abandonment to his will must absorb all else in me or, rather, transform and sublimate all the desires of my lower nature. (*JS*, 10 April 1903)

330 We will always be more joyful if the Lord is with us, and this is as true for the natural order as it is for the supernatural. In this way you will never want for patience towards your brothers and sisters: bearing with one another in joy. (9 January 1963)

331 Sadness and discontent take hold of me and I become agitated. Away with all these weaknesses! We must keep cheerful and calm, in all circumstances. Indeed, we must rejoice, since that is God's will.

(*JS*, 10 April 1903)

332 The Christian life is the will of God, which we can come to know to a sublime degree in the Gospel. This good news completely turns the earthly way of judging things and events on its head.

(22 February 1963)

333 Work away in charity and peace, knowing that nothing of all that we do in conformity to God's will, can ever be wasted on this earth.   (9 July 1959)

334 My soul is open before you, like a blank sheet of paper. Write on it what you will, O Lord: I am yours.   (*JS*, 10 April 1903)

PRAISE

But I will hope continually,
and will praise you yet more and more.
My mouth will tell of your righteous acts,
of your deeds of salvation all day long,
though their number is past my knowledge.
(Ps 71:14-15)

335 The life of the soul is like a song.
(28 February 1962)

336 In the days of rejoicing, let us bless the Lord! In the days of trial and sadness, let us offer thanksgiving to the Lord! For we know that it is the Lord who supports us through his help, his friendship, and his forgiveness. (29 October 1960)

337 Let us thank the Lord for all the blessings of his creation, let us praise him for having given us intelligence so that we can think, and hands so that we can work, and let us ask that he help us to carry out our work for the service of all in peace. (20 August 1961)

338 We are to do works of love, not deeds of hatred.
(14 October 1962)

339 All dangers and sorrows, all human wisdom and prudence, must dissolve into a canticle of love.
(28 October 1962)

340 Everyone, but everyone, needs to bless the Lord, since from every situation, every circumstance, we can receive not just a glimpse of charity, but charity itself with its burning flame. (8 May 1962)

341 The Lord could have given me the blessings of fortune, of wealth, or he could have withheld them – I had no right to them. He was pleased to withhold them. Why should I complain? Their absence is a means of sanctification. So, blessed be the name of the Lord. (*JS*, 10 April 1903)

342 The canticle of thanksgiving recognises all the blessings by which the Lord has supported us throughout our lives; it fills us with fresh energy to continue our path, with our gaze fixed always on the mercy and the kindness of the Lord.

(31 December 1961)

343 All our actions, all that we feel, pray, and do, must be as a most lofty hymn so that we give thanks and praise to Jesus Christ, to his charity, and to the example that he gave us. And so may our life here below be truly worthy of him and carry us to eternal life in our blessed homeland. (25 July 1962)

344 Besides this feeling of satisfaction, and this sense of my need for forgiveness, I feel gratitude too. Everything, O Lord, has been done for your glory: I thank you for it now and always. (*JS*, 10 August 1914)

FAITHFULNESS

Your word is a lamp to my feet,
and a light to my path.
I have sworn an oath and confirmed it,
to observe your righteous ordinances.

(Ps 119:105-106)

345 Do not let yourselves be oppressed by the spirit of the world, by the materialism that clips the wings of our spirit's holy energies, but be firm in your desire to remain faithful to God and his Church.

(23 April 1961)

346 The most valuable qualities or privileges that the human person possesses are charity, peace, repentance, work, and an unassailable sincerity towards God and man, a sure source of all well-being.

(20 September 1962)

347 God has inscribed his law on the human heart; he made it known to us through the revelation he made to Moses. It is a law which demands much and can sometimes seem rather hard. But the blessed Jesus, the Redeemer of the world, has come amongst us: and he has explained it to us, sweetened it; he has given it a new colour which has made it fascinating and attractive. This law is the law of love, of forgiveness, and of discretion in judgement; it is the law that makes us obliging to others, as long as this does not involve violating the Lord's Commandments.

(11 September 1960)

348 Whoever claims to be a Christian and tramples the Lord's Commandments underfoot, neither makes their own life holy, nor are they worthy of God.

(25 July 1962)

349 Yesterday, today, always: we have always to fight to remain firm in faith and charity, and if we do not wish to fall prey to the enticements of this passing life and become too comfortable. (6 April 1961)

350 It is not always heroic acts that are needed. A life which is a continual offering in the service of Christ, his Church, and souls is enough to ensure our sanctification and glory, without risking our lives on alpine peaks. (8 November 1953)

351 Work in Christ's name, and in his spirit; fulfil your duties; be faithful to God's teaching; suffer, if that is what is required: but always with the great certainty that the splendour of the Resurrection shines beyond your sufferings. So lives the true follower of the Gospel. (20 March 1960)

352 When we are faithful to the vocation to which the Lord has called us, truly faithful, with seriousness, ardour, energy, we are sure to receive the true consolations of life. (22 January 1963)

353 Be faithful to the letter of the law, but even more so to its spirit; it is the law you knowingly accepted. (13 June 1962)

354 The true Christian, who serves only one master and walks on the right path, has nothing to fear.

(11 September 1960)

355 Let our actions always be guided by the joy in our hearts, and the wisdom in our hearts and minds. Let us have a firm resolve to respond to God's continued entreaties, as he calls us to return to his light, which shines more brightly than any other light, and to his unchanging rule. (18 July 1962)

356 If anyone has unhappily distanced themselves from the Divine Redeemer through sin, let them return to him who is the way, the truth, and the life. If anyone is tepid, weak, and neglectful of their religious duties, let them stir up their faith and nourish and consolidate their virtues with the help of divine grace. In short, if someone is just, let them become even more just, if someone is holy, let them become even more holy. (26 September 1959)

357 Let us be sure to remain deeply united with Christ, the source of light and grace, who every day renews our spirits in joyfulness. (12 November 1955)

TRUST

And why do you worry about clothing?
Consider the lilies of the field and how they grow:
they neither toil nor spin,
yet I tell you, even Solomon in all his glory
was not clothed like one of these.

(Mt 6:28-29)

358 The word of Christ endures, it remains whole and unshakeable: 'Have trust, I have overcome the world!' No, thanks be to God, atheistic and materialistic conceptions of life will never have the weather gauge, they will never prevail. (4 November 1959)

359 Let us never abandon ourselves to melancholy; it wrongs the wisdom of our faith and the promises of the Lord. (8 December 1957)

360 Whoever has received from God the most wonderful gift of baptism need fear no evil.

(29 October 1960)

361 The Lord's hands are good, secure; we must entrust ourselves to them for there we will be completely secure. (14 December 1960)

362 With the help of grace all is possible in our search for true greatness, heroic enthusiasm, and holiness. (8 July 1962)

363 Courage! God cannot die, and Christ, the Son of God, will never break his promises. The Lord's grace is with us; and with this grace we can tackle any struggle that comes our way.   (23 February 1955)

364 All our days are in the hands of God. And since life and mercy come gushing from this fountain, we should not allow ourselves to be disturbed on any account whatsoever.   (25 November 1962)

365 Those souls who are disheartened have a tendency to see the earth as covered in nothing but darkness. We, on the other hand, love to reaffirm our faith in the Saviour, who did not leave the world which he redeemed.   (25 December 1961)

366 There are, of course, songs of great sadness. But there are also hymns of great rejoicing and happiness. In the midst of the trials that are never lacking let every person repeat their song of complete abandonment to God's will; and they can be sure that there is no tear that the Lord does not see, nor sigh that comes from a heart wrung by sacrifice that the Lord has not noticed.   (8 August 1962)

367 All is in the hands of God, and faith is of the greatest value, since it brings us tremendous well being.   (20 September 1962)

368 Lamentations resolve absolutely nothing. We need to keep going, to anticipate, and to have faith.
                    (2 July 1962)

369 The future is in God's hands. It spreads out, full of promise, before anyone who is resolved to work with the utmost faithfulness right to the very end, to

work with humble and prudent patience in the field belonging to the one and only father of the harvest.

(20 January 1963)

370 We must put aside our restlessness, impatience, and inability to put up with those unpleasant things which happen. The meaning of Christianity lies in serenity, interior quiet, and abandonment to God.

(11 September 1960)

371 It is well said that our sins are the seat of divine mercy. It is even better said that God's most beautiful name and title is this: mercy. This must inspire us with a great trust amid our tears.

(*JS*, 26 November 1940)

372 Do not let the difficulties we daily encounter in our work make you lose heart, but learn how to infuse your work with the generosity and enthusiasm that are born from your highest convictions.

(4 December 1960)

373 We must never feel saddened by the very straitened circumstances in which we live; we must be patient, look above and think of paradise.

(*JS*, 16 January 1901)

VOCATION

And he said to them,
'Follow me, and I will make you fish for people.'
Immediately they left their nets
and followed him.

(Mt 4:19-20)

374 Christ's voice resounds even now through out the world. With a gentle strength he draws all those to follow him who wish through prayer, apostolic service, and suffering to become those who fascinate and enthral souls. (16 December 1961)

375 In all the different tasks that Providence has entrusted to us, learn how to respond truly to your vocation and give an example of prompt adhesion to the will of the Divine Master. (8 July 1962)

376 We are all together, each one of us in our own street. Perhaps we were not expecting to be in this particular street, but the Lord's light shines on it nevertheless. (3 January 1959)

377 Let us return to the right path, according to the different circumstances in which Divine Providence has placed us. Praise and bless the Lord always.

(2 April 1961)

378 Follow the voice of the Lord, which calls us to rediscover our own lives; dedicate your life to Christ and the Gospel. (16 December 1961)

379 In our vocation we lose ourselves in order to find ourselves. We give – to him who repays a hundredfold now in this age and in the age to come eternal life (cf Mk 10:17) – our energies of soul and body, our talents and abilities for the coming of his Kingdom.

(16 December 1961)

380 The harvest is plentiful, but the labourers are few. In many regions apostles, exhausted by their labours, wait expectantly for their replacements. Entire peoples are suffering from a spiritual hunger which is far deeper than the material one; who will bring the heavenly nourishment of truth and life to them?

(1 August 1955)

381 Let labourers of the third hour, the sixth, the ninth, or even the eleventh hour, who are not familiar with this work, come to my vineyard, to the vineyard where Christ calls all, the young, the mature, and the old. There is a place for everyone. There is always work to be done, by day and by night; everything is done in the light, in justice, and in the spirit of the true brotherhood and sisterhood which has been sealed by the sacrifice and the blood of Christ.   (29 January 1956)

382 We can respond to God's invitation at any age: some give their lives to the Lord in childhood and serve him all their lives; for others it can be like lightning striking unexpectedly in the full vigour of their years, as it were upon a mystical road to Damascus. For God, the length of years is not important, what counts is the love with which we respond to him and serve him.   (20 October 1960)

383 The religious vocation is the joyful response of the soul to God's choice. The desire to belong to him alone and to serve him in a hidden life, it then becomes something which is of the greatest benefit to souls.

(11 May 1961)

HOLINESS

Instead, as he who called you is holy,
be holy yourselves in all your conduct;
for it is written,
'You shall be holy, for I am holy.'
(1 Pt 1:15)

384 The most important thing is to lead a holy life. This option is open to all, since the Lord has given us the energy, the youth, the strength, the opportunity, a mind to see and discern, and a heart to love. For each one of us the path is marked out clearly ahead.

(14 June 1961)

385 Sanctity must be the luminous goal of every follower of Christ, whatever their origin and their work, and in whatever forms of life they live or in whatever activity they are involved. (14 June 1961)

386 If anyone calls themselves a Christian, but does not strive to become holy, they bear a name which has no value for them. (25 July 1962)

387 The Lord invites all of us to live an ordered and holy life, since we are made in his image and likeness: 'Be holy, as I am holy' (Lev 11:44). Here lies the perfection and the joy of humankind and of the Christian. (24 January 1960)

388 The holiness of the saints is not founded on tremendous things, but on the tiniest of things that seem to the world to be nothing but trifles.

(*JS*, 10 April 1903)

389 What counts is the present moment, and that alone. (11 November 1962)

390 The path of virtue is arduous, but the summit to which it leads is bathed in light and there we find great recompense. (25 February 1961)

391 What counts is that we continue on our way, and that we work. We may very well be lacking or inadequate, but what matters is that we know how to work at our shortcomings and to continue diligently on our way. This is our intention, and the grace that the Lord concedes to us helps us to achieve that goal. And Christ, always and above all, desires it; Christ who is the truth, the goodness, and the beauty of our souls and of our lives. (7 October 1959)

392 The saints reached perfection by taking the road to Calvary, thus showing unfailing patience in the depths of their hearts. (26 February 1963)

393 Nothing is everything. These simple words contain a programme of life that is perfectly ascetical; total denial of self, faithfulness to grace, and zeal without limits. (2 December 1961)

394 Be a faithful image of God crucified, who gave his blood to illuminate the human path, and to nourish and heal humanity. (5 October 1962)

395 The fact that the saints survived at all is more wondrous even than their lives themselves. Throughout their lives they gave no thought as to whether God or other people misunderstood them. So it was with Jesus. (26 July 1953)

396 Wherever the saints passed, they left something of God. God always makes his presence felt: the soul recovers itself, and, as if brushed by the eternal, welcomes the leaven of the spiritual life.

(10 September 1955)

397 In the twenty centuries that have already passed, millions and millions of souls have preferred the poetry of the Cross to the attractions of the world and of the flesh. (26 March 1955)

398 In the spiritual field there is a constant progression of lights, of colours, and of clear and vast horizons. (9 September 1961)

399 God and souls, the inner life and the apostolate, love of God and of our neighbour: the surest of hinges, on which hangs the story of every saint and which proclaim the irresistible fascination of their example in the sight of the world. (11 May 1961)

400 It is God's desire that, following the example of the saints, we might absorb from them the vital essence of virtue, converting it into our own blood and adapting it to our own particular dispositions and special circumstances. (*JS*, 16 January 1903)

401 There is only one way to holiness, but the actual paths that lead there are many. (8 May 1955)

PRAYER

Pray without ceasing,
give thanks in all circumstances;
for this is the will of God
in Christ Jesus for you.
(1 Thess 5:17)

402 Contemplate and love, so that you may immerse yourself in God in your search to discern his will. (29 April 1961)

403 The soul breathes through prayer. Unfortunately, in the spiritual order of things the world does appear to be rather unhappy. Among the few of us mortals who actually pray, there are fewer still who know how to pray well. (11 February 1958)

404 So, here again more calm. Prayers may be few in number but they must be said composedly, at least as well as if I were talking to my fellows.
(*JS*, 6 September 1900)

405 We need to leave behind every earthly preoccupation when it is time to talk with God and to draw closer to him. (14 December 1960)

406 Let prayer be the air you breathe, and your nourishment. (17 October 1959)

407 Let your prayer be inspired by an ardent and persevering faith. Let it be accompanied by that Christian penance that renders it more acceptable to God, and more effective. (25 December 1961)

408 Prayer and penance are the two wings which lift the soul up and allow it to rise towards God.

(1 September 1962)

409 Anyone who wishes to progress in prayer requires a searching self-knowledge and severe self-mortification, and the concupiscence of the flesh must be watched over and promptly mortified.

(6 January 1956)

410 Let your prayer be continuous, thoughtful, and wise. May it be your nourishment, may it be like the air you breathe that keeps you alive, protecting you from the stench of a worldly attitude.

(28 January 1960)

411 Your prayer must be watered from the springs of a profound knowledge of Sacred Scripture, above all the New Testament, and then by the liturgy and the teaching of the Church in all its fullness. (2 July 1962)

412 Charity and prayer support each other. If a thirst for charity does not rouse our prayer, then it falters or ceases altogether. (6 January 1956)

413 Greater importance must be given to inner rather than outward activity, since the supernatural life which nourishes the soul comes from the inner person.

(27 February 1962)

414 Without prayer our actions become something merely external and inconclusive, hiding their emptiness and fruitlessness under ephemeral achievements. Without prayer sacrifice cannot attain its real value, since it becomes harsh and cold.

(3 November 1961)

415 Only through persistence in prayer are we able to receive the strength that comes down from heaven.

(26 September 1959)

416 When the human person withdraws into themselves they meet God. In this withdrawal we can draw on the energies necessary to overcome evil, to give a supernatural meaning to all that goes on around us, and to bring our lives ever nearer to the ideals of grace and charity to which we aspire.　　(8 August 1962)

417 When Christians call upon God they ask that all might receive light, the clarity of good ideas, and good principles by which to live.

(16 September 1959)

418 The prayer of innocent souls purifies the world and calls down divine grace upon the earth.

(24 September 1959)

419 Pure prayer flows from a conscience that is serene and at peace. Pure prayer listens to God, it speaks with him, it rests silently in him, and it asks what pleases him. It is a prayer of adoration and thanksgiving, rather than of petition. The Lord knows of what we have need.　　(29 January 1960)

420 The life we lead when we have given ourselves to the Lord has its difficulties and requires sacrifices, just as any other form of life does. Prayer alone can obtain the gift of perseverance.　　(2 July 1962)

421 The 'Our Father' is a perfect summary of a philosophy of life by which every soul, and every people can live, in any age, past, present, and future.

(4 November 1961)

422 When evening comes and you are returning home, pause a while in prayer, so that the Spirit may speak to your soul in the silence, and flood it with his heavenly light. (31 May 1959)

423 A day without prayer is like a sky devoid of the sun, or a garden without flowers. (4 May 1963)

PENANCE

Always carrying in the body
the death of Jesus,
so that the life of Jesus
may also be made visible in our bodies.

(2 Cor 4:10)

424 This and nothing else is the reality: there can be no human person without discipline, and there can be no Christian without penance. (15 February 1959)

425 Not all are called to extraordinary and difficult forms of voluntary mortification, but every Christian must practise penance by keeping a check on the tongue, the stomach, the senses, and pride. Every Christian must practise self-denial.   (20 October 1960)

426 The joy of one who is mortified is of purely heavenly origin.   (*JS*, 18 December 1903)

427 We receive consolations in our lives in the measure to which we are able to divest ourselves of everything and have no other preoccupation than to realise in ourselves the perfection of the 'Our Father' and the doctrine that it contains and exalts.

(19 March 1955)

428 There are two doors to paradise: innocence and penance. Poor and fragile as we are, who can hope to find the first open to them? The second, however, is certainly open, and Jesus passed through it, with the cross on his shoulders, in expiation of our sins, and he invites us to follow him. But to follow him means we must do penance, allow ourselves to be scourged, and to scourge ourselves a little, too.   (*JS*, 27 June 1957)

429 God can be found in the detachment from every earthly hindrance, in those who truly seek the Lord's will and his glory.   (29 April 1961)

430 The first external penance that all must do is to accept from God with a trusting and resigned soul all the suffering and sorrows that we encounter in our lives, and all the toil and the trouble that comes to us from the exact fulfilment of the duties of our state, daily work, and exercise of the Christian virtues.

(1 July 1962)

431 Unfortunately human fragility does not understand the law of sacrifice that unites us intimately with the patient Christ and allows us to share in his divine nature.   (23 February 1955)

432 If we wish to be of Jesus, to belong to him on this earth and in the blessed eternity of heaven, then we must follow him: we must take up the cross and carry it with him, behind him; we must discipline our nature, wounded by sin, so that the new self, created by God 'in justice and true holiness' (Eph 4:24), might triumph.   (3 April 1960)

433 It is only human to make mistakes, but we must immediately get up again and mend our ways.

(16 November 1960)

434 If we are not at peace with our conscience, then tranquillity and inner joy will be lacking.

(31 January 1962)

435 If the outward works of penance are not accompanied by inner purity of soul and sincere repentance for sins, then they are vain. (1 July 1962)

436 When I have committed some sin or feel distressed, I shall imagine myself kneeling at the foot of the cross, like Mary Magdalene, and receiving on my head the shower of blood and water which flowed from the Saviour's wounded Heart. (*JS*, 10 April 1903)

437 You will of course remember that touching depiction, of which art offers many examples, of the shepherd who is carrying the lost lamb upon his shoulders. The shepherd's hands are all bloody, because he had had to take the lamb from the thorns, but joy shines in his eyes. (28 February 1954)

438 All those who have besmirched their white baptismal robe with grave faults ought greatly to fear God's chastisement, unless they strive to make themselves white and splendid once more in the blood of the Lamb through the Sacrament of Penance and the practise of Christian virtues. (1 July 1962)

439 Lets us put this right, once and for all. Until now I have done nothing but play around with God. But one does not play around with God.

(*JS*, 28 March 1897)

440 Even though your gaze may be constantly directed heavenwards, you might still find that your shoes or your clothes become covered by the dust of this age to a greater or lesser extent. This could affect your attempts at living the good life or following the way of perfection. Whatever the case, when there is sin, there is a necessity for penance. (3 March 1960)

441 Whether things up to now have gone well or badly, let us begin another round immediately.

(JS, 1 April 1903)

442 What joy there is in being pardoned, what consolation there is on leaving the conversation with your father confessor, which you had entered upon with humility and confidence, and hearing him say: 'Go, my child, courage, set out once more on your path with all good will, I absolve you of your sins'.

(17 April 1963)

443 Thanks to God's infinite mercy we can rise once more from a state of sin. But the very worst we can do is to persist in evil ways and believe that we can force God to forgive us just like that, as if he were inconstant just as we are. (16 November 1960)

444 O blessed penance, which can and must become for us a fountain of ineffable graces. O blessed suffering, which in union with Christ and his blessed Mother is destined to become for us a cause of eternal delight and glory. (11 February 1958)

SIMPLICITY

I thank you, Father,
Lord of heaven and earth,
because you have hidden these things
from the wise and the intelligent
and have revealed them to infants.

(Lk 10:21)

445 Whoever is able to become like a child is great in the Kingdom of Heaven. The innocence and the affectionate nature of a child draws us, attracts us, and cheers us up. (11 October 1959)

446 If we do not become like children, that is, if we do not preserve within ourselves the enchantment of purity and simplicity (first in our attitude and then in the practice of all the virtues), then we will not be able to enter the Kingdom of Heaven. (23 August 1961)

447 Simplicity may cause, I don't say scorn, but a lack of consideration on the part of those who think themselves wise. But such people are of no account; even if their opinions and conduct inflict some humiliations, no notice should be taken of them at all: in the end everything ends in their defeat and confusion. The 'simplex et rectus ac timens', 'simple, upright, God-fearing man' (Job 1:1), is always the worthiest and the strongest. (*JS*, 13 August 1961)

448 God's goodness is beautiful and wonderful beyond compare. It is enough that our hearts be turned towards him because, although he is silent, the Lord sees inside our heart and fills it with his grace.

(24 September 1959)

449 Simplicity contains nothing contrary to prudence, and the converse also is true. Simplicity is love: prudence is thought. Love prays: intelligence keeps watch. 'Watch and pray' (Mt 26:41): a perfect harmony. Love is like the cooing dove; active intelligence is like the snake that never falls to the ground or bruises itself, because it first probes with its head to test the unevenness of the ground before it glides along.

(*JS*, 13 August 1961)

450 The Lord loves to perform his wonderful deeds where he finds a foundation of simplicity, that is, where there is a renunciation of all human scheming and a sincere and confident desire to do what divine grace inspires and will carry out.   (1 September 1961)

451 He is a simple man who is not ashamed to profess the Gospel, even in the face of men who consider it nothing but weakness and childish nonsense, and to profess it entirely, on all occasions, and in the presence of all; he does not let himself be deceived or prejudiced by his fellows, nor does he lose his peace of mind, however they may treat him.

(*JS*, 13 August 1961)

452 Let us remain obedient, with the Gospel in our hands and peace in our hearts through the grace of God, in perfect simplicity and humility right to the very end.   (5 November 1955)

HUMILITY

Who, though he was in the form of God,
did not regard equality with God
as something to be exploited,
but emptied himself,
taking the form of a slave,
being born in human likeness.

(Phil 2:6-7)

453 My dear, you must learn to lower that head of yours, so full of vanities, and to think humbly of yourself, otherwise you will stumble along blindly and fall down. (*JS*, 1898)

454 There is another virtue which is a perennial source of joy and true optimism: humility, which feeds on the truth and is anchored in confidence in God.

(18 March 1959)

455 If we want to scale the heights we must never forget that the path which leads there is humility. Humility comes before glory. The higher a building soars, the deeper the foundations must be.

(7 May 1962)

456 'Learn from me, for I am gentle and lowly in heart' (Mt 11:29). Take note: this is the foundation, the great foundation of Christian life. I would go even further: the foundation of perfection and holiness.

(15 February 1958)

457 Humility scales down the image that we have of ourselves to its true proportions, according to the law of reason. (7 May 1962)

458 The recognition of one's own limits is the starting point for every spiritual conquest, in the spiritual order as in the order of grace. (19 March 1959)

459 Gentleness and humility are not simply two flowers that merely add to the beauty of nature. They are the very roots of the tree: the reason why God's field blooms so wonderfully and so richly. (15 February 1958)

460 Learn from Jesus, the Son of God, not to create the world, nor to launch the stars on their swift and luminous course, nor to govern peoples and determine their fate: but to be gentle and humble of heart. (4 October 1953)

461 When we humble ourselves, God comes to our aid. (*JS*, 24 July 1898)

462 Humility is the true claim to glory for us who dwell here below, because it implies the recognition of God's rights, the sincere acceptance of Christ's precepts, and the generous dedication to the service of the human family. (10 May 1963)

463 Neither arrogance nor pride will ever produce the right conditions, where a deeply felt brotherhood and sisterhood can flourish. (7 November 1962)

464 Jesus did not say to us: 'Learn from me that I am the Son of the heavenly Father'; he did not teach us to create the heavens and the earth, or to clothe the sun in his shining mantle, but how to be gentle and humble of heart. Here is the very foundation of goodness. If we are filled with it, our progress through life will be all the more secure and we will be better able to overcome the obstacles and miseries of this earthly life. (20 March 1960)

465 At the foot of the cross, on which the Divine Victim was sacrificed, grows humility – the first Christian virtue, without which all the other virtues grow weak. (15 September 1958)

466 When I feel oppressed, abandoned, alone, I will bow my head, be satisfied, and say: 'This I deserve, may it be so.' (*JS*, 18 April 1903)

467 For the Christian, the thought of being a sinner does not by any means signify that we should lose heart. What it does mean is that we must have a confident and habitual trust in the Lord Jesus who has redeemed and forgiven us. We must have a keen sense of respect for other people and their souls and be on our guard against the danger of becoming proud of our achievements. (*JS*, 26 November 1940)

468 When I have been faithful to my intentions, my heart praises my God, for he has done everything. When I fail, I guard closely against discouragement. (*JS*, 20 December 1902)

469 I must learn to face it, this judgment of others, to cast it aside and ignore it. (*JS*, 18 December 1903)

470 We are all poor before the Lord. (8 August 1962)

The
human person
and life

LIFE

Whoever has the Son has life;
whoever does not have the Son of God,
does not have life.

(1 Jn 5:12)

471 Life is a song sung well and harmoniously with all skill that the Lord has given us, and with all that he has provided for us for our good. (28 February 1962)

472 In life it does not matter whether the things you do are great or small, wonderful or insignificant, but whether you do them with love, seeking God's will, even during times of suffering or trial.

(31 May 1959)

473 We should see life as a duty to be fulfilled, not as a pleasure to conquer and enjoy. (23 February 1955)

474 There is no doubt that money must be used if our lives are to be peaceful and ordered, but it must be seen as a means to good and viewed in the infinite light that comes from God himself, from God who is the author of prosperity and who gives his gifts unstintingly to nature and to humankind. (18 June 1961)

475 Life, even the life of a good Christian, is an unceasing renewal of self, in which we must continually start afresh. (1 December 1957)

476 What is important is that we move on and never to get stuck in the furrows of our settled habits, that we are constantly on the lookout for new contacts, and that we remain open to the genuine needs of the time in which we have been called to live, so that Christ might be announced and known in all ways.

(20 March 1960)

477 In giving us time, God has entrusted something of great value to humankind. We must use it for his glory and the complete perfection of the human person.

(26 August 1962)

478 Life has not been given us so that we become closed within ourselves, in egoism and frivolity, but to become larger in stature, to build up, and to do good. We must not be inert, lazy, or paralysed, but generous and ardent. (29 September 1960)

479 The true Christian, who has made the teaching and example of St Paul his own, has no idea of what it is to come to a halt or, even worse, to go backwards. But, full of joyful hope and the desire to make the world a better place and to become better themselves, the true Christian moves forward in peace, eagerly searching for what is good and striving to experience more deeply the most excellent dignity that belongs to them as a creature alive in Christ. True Christians wish their thoughts, affections, activities, and work be found worthy of Christ. (24 July 1960)

480 Life is all about service, and we should dedicate it to the one Lord and master. (11 September 1960)

481 Our lives as human beings are a continual journey, and everything that happens in them is a stage along the way that will, one day, lead us to the house of the Lord. (2 December 1961)

482 We must walk quickly beside God.

(7 November 1962)

483 Follow Christ throughout your life, whether it be short or long, happy or full of distress. This is what counts most of all. To each one their own life, and their own way. (1 January 1958)

484 Life, both human and Christian, is like a great procession in which all walk together under the Holy Cross, the same cross which Jesus himself carried.

(7 March 1962)

485 Life, both as human beings and Christians, is a great and mysterious thing: a succession and interweaving of joys, of sorrows, and of triumphs. Is it not so, my brothers and sisters? (2 October 1955)

486 Human life is sacred: from the very beginning God's creative action works directly on it. Violate its laws, and you offend his divine majesty, you degrade your own selves and humanity at large, and you sap the vigour from the community to which you belong.

(15 May 1961)

487 If you are young, take joy in the vigour of your age and your innocence. If you are old, take joy in the riches of experience. And finally, if you are very advanced in age, you may, in the certainty that the world will not end, withdraw in peace, so that others may continue along the good path which you have already taken and continue to perform the good works that you have already accomplished. (19 July 1961)

488 'God sees me': our humble grandmothers used to work this motto into their samplers of rustic embroidery: they still hang on the old walls of our houses and contain a great reminder, which serves to give a character of decency to all our actions.

(JS, 27 November 1940)

489 Life is full of consolations, above all, for those who remain united spiritually to the Gospel and the Lord's grace. *(15 April 1956)*

490 Our whole lives should be a song, a song that contains within it a great range of expression. And the more open it is to what is precious in God's sight, the more elevated it will be. *(18 July 1962)*

491 Human life becomes meaningful when it chooses God as the ultimate aim of all its aspirations.

(16 August 1959)

JOY

Rejoice in the Lord always;
again I will say, Rejoice.
(Phil 4:4)

492 For the Christian even the setting sun has an enduring brilliance. (19 March 1959)

493 Be joyful, keep well, you may even accept every legitimate amusement that life offers, but never fail to have God's law before you, in every event, in every moment. And remember that the Cross is with us always, we have it today, and it will not be absent tomorrow. (26 February 1961)

494 Those who believe themselves to be happy while dedicating themselves to the pleasant but passing things of the world alone and give no thought to the rest, to what is essential and eternal, are playing a game that will turn out to be very short-lived.
(13 November 1958)

495 Let us take courage, and rejoice in the Lord. This is the medicine that quietens all our impatience, sweetens our privations, and makes us full of joy, even when we are experiencing life's bitterness.
(*JS*, 20 December 1902)

496 It is true indeed that anyone who thinks regularly of Paradise is always joyful, and that they find in this thought the strength to pass over all the miseries of the human state and to direct all the energies they possess to the practice of those virtues of which Jesus himself was master: meekness, and humility in spirit, in word, and on the features of their face.

(17 October 1958)

497 Joy places the soul in direct communication with the Lord.   (18 July 1962).

498 *Amour-propre* paralyses the growth of the spirit and fills us with sadness. Mortification restores life, serenity, and peace.   (*JS*, 18 December 1903)

499 We must be very careful of our joy, so as to keep our spirit mortified. And we must practise mortification, in order to increase our joy.

(*JS*, 18 December 1903)

500 History always teaches us that joy of heart is the one, true joy, and that the profound and most intimate joy that comes from it can remain intact even in the midst of the most acute suffering.

(26 February 1961)

501 Seek joy, carrying with you wherever you go a note of sincerity, of uprightness, avoiding anything that hints of deceitfulness or laziness. Do this so that a spring of living water might come pouring out of your life, and its waters will reach as far as eternal life.

(18 December 1958)

YOUTH

I write to you, young people,
because you are strong,
and the word of God abides in you,
and you have overcome the evil one.

(1 Jn 2:14)

502 The Church says to the young: 'Do not allow yourselves to be carried away by anxiety. The Lord accompanies you along the road. He will help you, so that you will do good and distinguish yourselves.'

(23 July 1960)

503 When one asks for everything, one receives much. The young are generous. They are not content to remain where they are, but are anxious to know and to go deeply into things. (1 June 1962)

504 Do not distance yourself, beloved young people, from the justly optimistic vision that ought to guide your steps. Be people of peace, be builders of peace, everyone of you. (1 June 1962)

505 Life is a realisation of a youthful dream. Each one of you should have your own dream so that you can make it a most wonderful reality. A dream of generosity, of uprightness, of a certain loftiness, of a resolution to do good, to give yourself, to build up. Faithfulness to a way of behaving that is always pure and always honest. (20 May 1960)

506 The feelings of discouragement and destructive pessimism, which often dissipate energies that are still vigorous, have not tarnished the clear crystal of your youth. (17 September 1961)

507 Take courage. Love one another. Get in touch with reality and aim for what is essential. And never let respect for outward forms suffocate the beating of your hearts. (26 May 1962)

508 Be young, and so be open to all that is beautiful, holy, and just. (17 September 1961)

509 The age of youth is marked by three main characteristic gifts: joy, wisdom, and strength, expressed with courage and dignity. (18 July 1962)

510 If a young person is not full of joy, they indeed appear truly desolate. (18 July 1962)

511 Blessed are you, young people, because you are strong. Strength is the distinguishing characteristic of youth. While the rest of us would begin our list of the cardinal virtues with prudence, for the youth one can and must put the accent on strength. (20 May 1960)

512 The young will never learn to be masters of themselves if they do not learn lovingly to observe a firm rule of life which will teach them mortification and the mastery of the will.

(9 September 1962)

513 The young always think that they know more than their elders. They do not like to hear the observations of others, and they do not readily accept advice. It is an old story, and one that will repeat itself for the old people of tomorrow. What retains a lasting value for today and tomorrow is experience, wisdom, discretion, and, above all, a willingness to accept the guidance of the Church. (9 June 1956)

514 When you think of your mothers you feel a sense of pride and affection. This thought expresses the esteem and love that you have for your family, and your family sustains you in your resolution to remain worthy of your earthly and eternal vocation.

(20 May 1960)

515 You are the guarantee of peace and the hope for better times. Why? Because on your foreheads shine three noble characteristics: you are young, you are willing, and you are dedicated.   (17 September 1961)

516 We have a firm trust that the youth of our time will not be less generous in responding to the Master's call than were the youth of times past.

(1 August 1959)

517 As he did to the youth in the Gospel, Jesus invites you too to be generous. For some of you, who are called to more sublime ideals, perhaps it is a question of putting into practice the words of the Gospel: 'Go, sell all that you own and distribute the money to the poor, and you will have treasure in heaven; then come, follow me' (Mt 19:21).

(20 September 1960)

518 When you are young life smiles on you, and instead of frightening you, its difficulties spur you on to overcome them.   (3 November 1961)

519 Let the young people, who give such great hope to the Church, know that in their life's journey they will encounter the Cross and sometimes even deep anxiety. But since these young people are Christians they know that, in God's most wonderful plan, every single tear that escapes from our eyes and every single sigh from our hearts contributes to true peace here below and boundless joy in eternity. (6 August 1960)

520 Preserve transparency and courage in confronting the most difficult trials. Preserve also your preoccupation with all that is good in life.
(17 September 1961)

521 The young pay no attention to fatigue and habit. (1 June 1962)

522 When the young understand how to fulfil their duty to God and the Church then they truly become living messengers of uprightness, serenity, and peace.
(29 July 1961)

523 In the serenity and order of your youth, young people, lies the secret of the peaceful development of society that awaits you. (17 September 1961)

524 Be the living stones of the cities in which you live, my dear children and young people. Be true witnesses to the gifts that God showers on you and all your worthy fellow citizens. This you should do through your religious cultural values and the job that you do, but above all through the uprightness of your character, of your intentions, and your actions.
(26 April 1961)

525 The young need no more than Jesus' presence beside them to satisfy their deepest aspirations. But the extent to which these aspirations are satisfied depends on each person's ability to open themselves up and look their own greatness and miseries straight in the eye. (2 June 1962)

526 Animated by a living faith, by faithfulness to prayer, and with an inner life enriched through communion with Jesus in the Eucharist – the way, the truth, and the life – the young know how to give witness. They know how to be, through their example, the channel that carries many souls who have become distanced from God to the doctrine of life they have been hoping for in great anxiety.   (21 April 1963)

527 The young people of today can feel a life-giving breath passing over them. This breath stimulates both their esteem for the goods of the Spirit and their desire to acquire them.   (23 June 1962)

528 We are currently witnessing everywhere a striving for perfection, not only in terms of organisation and technology but also in spiritual matters, and in every sector of economic, political, and cultural life, as well as in sport and recreation. And this situation would seem to allow us to make a more optimistic evaluation of young people today than we could have in the past.
(16 September 1962)

529 What trepidation a young life must cause as it stands at the very beginning of its journey, facing so many unknowns – but supported so sweetly by our heavenly Father's hand.   (14 July 1961)

530 Spring is in perfect harmony with youth.
(29 March 1962)

531 There are some worrying voices to be heard who question the consistency of today's youth. We pay no heed to them.   (17 September 1961)

532 Youth is a song.   (18 July 1962)

FAMILY

'Honour your father and your mother':
this is the first commandment
with a promise:
'so that it may be well with you
and you may live long on the earth.'
(Eph 6:2-3)

533 The family is a gift from God. As such it entails a vocation that comes from on high in which there is no room for any pretence or the mere acting of a role. In the family begins true and good education. The family is everything, or nearly everything, for humankind. (7 December 1960)

534 The real strength and robustness of all our villages, cities, and nations lies in those families which are based on a willingness to work, mutual respect, and the fear of God. Such families provide the foundation for every virtue, our defence against every danger of corruption, and a source of healthy and constantly renewed energies that work for the good of individuals and every form of civil association. (11 January 1959)

535 When the fireplaces are well alight and the grace of the Lord is at work, the most wonderful things happen to give witness to the supernatural and the divine, even through the humblest of circumstances.
(28 October 1959)

536 Jesus transformed water into wine at the wedding at Cana to show that in every family there is a

note of joy which sounds clear through all the confusion
and excessiveness. (10 January 1962)

537 In every good family's exercise of the virtues,
reciprocal love must burn like a flame. Goodness
sweetens and reinforces the father's authority, the
mother's sensitivity spreads it through the whole family,
while the same goodness gives meaning to the children's
obedience, is happy with their exuberance and inspires
them to accept the sacrifices that are never wanting.
(24 December 1961)

538 In the mind of the Church the true Christian
hearth is the place where a child's faith grows and
develops, and where children learn not only to become
adults but also a son or daughter of God.
(3 May 1959)

539 Determine to aim high in everything, always:
in the matter of purity and the defence of morality,
and the living and passing on of goodness, and in the
perfume of prayer. Aim high in all these things so that
the number of families who give honour to God's name
and are prompt to obey the will of the Divine Master
may increase. (8 July 1962)

540 Deep in the bosom of God lies eternal fruitfulness. Its active and benign reflection is found in
some way in the children of the human family, who
have been raised to the highest dignity and duties as
ancestors. (20 October 1960)

541 In those homes where children are awaited and
welcomed as precious gifts from God, the Kingdom

of Christ has nothing to fear; in those homes its fundamental laws are respected.   (25 October 1959)

542 It seems to me that those homes which contain large families provide a particularly visible witness to faithfulness to God and a very real example of abandonment to his providence.   (7 January 1962)

543 The child, with its innocence, is the first teacher in its own home.   (31 March 1963)

544 The presence of children makes it easy for us to have a bright and very rooted vision of the future.
(31 March 1963)

545 The Lord's grace is reflected in a child. This invites us to respect them and to prize the true value of their most wonderful characteristic: closeness to God.
(31 March 1963)

546 If we wanted to pick out one of the most marvellous and attractive features of life in the family, we would think of a little one's faltering words as it pronounced the words of its first prayer: the 'Hail Mary'. And nothing – it might rightly be observed – nothing is more beautiful and charming than a child's salutation to the Most Holy Virgin.
(8 September 1960)

547 Have great care for the innocence of your children so that throughout their lives they might always reflect God and be his living image.
(12 March 1963)

548 The religious and moral education of children, and their physical health, depends for a large part on the uprightness and integrity of their parents.

(10 January 1962)

549 Within the family, the father could almost be said to stand in God's place. He must lead and guide the other family members not through his authority alone, but also by the example of his honest life.

(29 June 1959)

550 A woman has an irreplaceable role in the family. When a woman knows how to make herself heard and respected hers is the voice that all listen to: the watchful and prudent voice of the woman, the spouse, and the mother.

(7 December 1960)

551 Your mission as mothers entrusts you with great responsibilities and requires great sacrifices. But when this mission is fulfilled properly in the light of the Gospel and the teachings of the Church it becomes a cause of great joy for the parents who see their children – flesh of their flesh – grow as temples of the Holy Spirit who dwells in them through grace.

(12 May 1963)

552 When a mother encourages, invites, and entreats the members of her family, her voice makes a profound and unforgettable impression in the depths of their hearts. Oh, only God knows what a stimulus for good this voice is, and of what great use it is to the Church and to human society.

(7 December 1960)

553 The mother, affectionate and good towards her

husband, should form her children firmly and graciously by the mildness of her manner and by her virtue. Together the parents should carefully rear their children, God's most precious gift, to an upright and religious life. (29 June 1959)

554 If Christian parents discover that a child of theirs has been blessed by a vocation to the priesthood or religious life, let them feel the greatness of this honour and encourage their child's response to God's voice in every way possible. (16 September 1959)

555 The secret of true peace, of an enduring and mutual accord, of the obedience of children, of the flowering of a gracious manner of behaving, lies in the continual and generous imitation of the sweetness, modesty, and gentleness found in the family of Nazareth. (10 January 1960)

556 Jesus Christ has given his meaning to marriage, raising this contract among the baptised to the level of a sacrament. Through being the member of a family, he wished also to make family life holy, a place where the most beautiful virtues are found.
(10 February 1959)

557 To us, Mary symbolises the most wonderful of all our families, the family of Nazareth.
(4 October 1962)

558 If families, though they are beset by the difficulties that life brings, knew how to safeguard jealously the precious heritage of a fully conscious and convinced faith, a faith that is luminous and ardent;

and if they knew how to draw from this faith the secret of a serenity that never fades, then, even today, society would have a greater stability and would be possessed of a sure defence.   (11 May 1961)

559 Have the desire to make of this unique and privileged society that is the family a true cell of the Church. A cell where God is honoured, above all through prayer together, where his holy law is observed, even though this may at times prove rather difficult. A cell where the most precious fruits of the human heart – the love between spouses, between parents and children, and between the children themselves – can grow harmoniously in love.   (3 May 1959)

WORK

We urge you, beloved,
to aspire to live quietly,
to mind your own affairs,
and to work with your hands.

(1 Thess 4:10-11)

560 Human work is sacred, because it is the action of a rational creature who has been raised to the dignity of a child of God. (19 April 1961)

561 God imprinted his image and likeness in the human person through the breath of the Spirit, and all that is produced through human agency should be given life by the same Spirit: the tools of agriculture, the marvellous machines of technology, and the instruments of research. (4 October 1962)

562 Anything that is of value can only be obtained through sweat and fatigue, and we ought to pity anyone who thinks differently, since to do so is to desire to place oneself outside the order created by Providence. (11 April 1962)

563 Work is something that has been entrusted to every member of the human race: it is the very foundation of life. (13 March 1963)

564 The human person is called to cooperate with the designs of God the Creator. All human endeavour, even the most humble, has been rendered noble and exalted through Jesus' labours in the workshop at Nazareth. (4 October 1962)

565 In our work we have been entrusted with a lofty mission: through it we collaborate in a real and intelligent way with God the Creator, from whom we have received the good things of the earth, in order to cultivate them and allow them to flourish. The tiring and difficult nature of our work is part of God's redeeming plan. God saved the world through the love and sufferings of his only Son, and so he rendered suffering into a precious tool of sanctification, if our suffering is united to that of Christ.   (1 May 1960)

566 It is a good and noble thing, as long as our strength permits us, to render our lives more beautiful through a daily resolve to work faithfully and to serve the truth and true Christian brotherhood and sister-hood. It is so much better than falling into apathy and cluttering up our lives with lamentations for times past, and wringing our hands over the storms we see threatening us, whether they be near at hand or far distant.   (10 September 1954)

567 Work has been made holy, blessed, and rendered glorious and splendid through the example of our Redeemer. So even here below we can taste an incomparable joy.   (5 March 1961)

568 During our earthly pilgrimage we have two choices: we can either work and all will be well with us, or we can fall into sadness and run the risk of languishing in the most serious and pernicious discomfort.   (5 March 1961)

569 Work is the source of true joy.
                    (21 March 1962)

570 Kindness is an indispensable condition of any work you do. Be gracious and full of charity. If you do so you will be successful as regards other people and gain merit in the eyes of God.   (31 May 1959)

571 Work ought not to be seen as a commodity and evaluated accordingly, but rather as an expression of the human person.   (15 May 1961)

572 True riches lie in work.   (21 August 1961)

573 Work that is well done tends to favour the growth of obedience, good order, and peace.
                              (21 March 1962)

574 Love the earth, that generous and severe mother, who holds in her womb all the treasures of Providence.
                              (22 April 1959)

575 If the love of the earth, the family, and the Church is alive in you, then the most wonderful peace imaginable will fill your hearts. God's blessings also will descend on you like the dew that freshens the fields in the morning and makes the flowers even more beautiful.   (22 June 1959)

576 I encourage you to do your work properly, with patience and sacrifice. Whatever service it is your duty to perform for society, do it in a spirit of charity.
                              (31 May 1959)

577 How wonderful it is to place every seed of devotion, everything we propose to do, and every one of our labours under the watchful eye of Mary, our Mother.   (5 February 1959)

578 May the most excellent Mother of God, who is present in the midst of all your labours and all your toil through the innumerable sanctuaries and hermitages which, like stars, add greatly to the beauty of your fields, look on you with favour, defend your life from every danger, make your land fruitful, and grant peace and prosperity to your homes.

(24 January 1959)

579 Blessed be the name of the Lord. He himself carries all the day's burdens.   (26 August 1962)

SUFFERING

My brothers and sisters,
whenever you face trials of any kind,
consider it nothing but joy,
because you know that the testing of your faith produces
endurance

(Jas 1:2-3)

580 Our pilgrimage here on earth is not of the kind whose path leads us across gardens, singing.

(15 March 1961)

581 If the Lord makes some jasmine, a rose, or some other beautiful flower shoot up between the thorns of this life, we must remember that such pleasures are really only little things and cannot give us true peace. They provide a respite, that is all.   (11 July 1958)

582 So Jesus too had his hour of despondency; he felt our human weaknesses. This is comfort to us who get discouraged over so little, and is a divine example for us to follow.   (*JS*, 20 December 1902)

583 The Church will inevitably encounter tribulation, opposition, and persecution. But the Master's words sound always in our hearts, 'Do not be afraid' (Mt 14:27). The Lord comes to our aid with his grace, especially in times of suffering.

(13 August 1960)

584 Life is always marked by suffering, and we will always be called to practise humility and patience. Everyone knows very well that it is impossible to avoid sorrow and affliction, for they are the vehicle that the Lord has given us to convey us safely to the fulfilment of his infallible promises. (6 July 1960)

585 Without sacrifice and suffering we would remain alone, as if we were in the desert. But through sacrifice and suffering we will always have Jesus.

(3 March 1957)

586 It is impossible to speak of Christianity without explicitly referring to voluntary sacrifice and mortification, and to the voluntary (and for this very reason, courageous) sharing of all here below in the suffering of their brothers and sisters, regardless of who they are. (22 January 1963)

587 Joy, the fruit of peace, is not ours to enjoy every day. Our heritage includes suffering also, even though we naturally wish to avoid it and are not inclined to put up with it in patience. And yet in spite of everything, we must accept it and make it holy.

(16 September 1961)

588 The gracious hand of God gives and takes away both great things and small: it is gracious still when it allows us to experience anxiety and to suffer.

(31 December 1957)

589 Carry around with you always the image of the suffering Christ. For in this same suffering lies the secret of life, of continuing along the way, of strength, of dignity, and of all those good works which nourish hope and the reward we await from God.

(1 February 1959)

590 Poverty has its thorns, and these we must love so that they become heaven's roses.   (2 July 1962)

591 I like very much to be in good health. And now I am ill. God has sent me this illness. Well then, may this illness be blessed.   (*JS*, 20 December 1902)

592 There are houses that have been visited by a crushing and overpowering need, and that have been tested by a profound lack of not only bread but also work, grief-stricken by the anxieties that a complete lack of a stable occupation generates.

(7 January 1962)

593 We often have trouble trying to understand and to perform our duty, but duty can become a tool of purification and redemption, sometimes even of heroism and holiness.   (2 September 1956)

594 There are houses whose silence contains illness, physical or moral suffering, or perhaps people who are spiritually lost.   (7 January 1962)

595 Among those who must bear illness there are some who understand the meaning of suffering, and consequently realise that they have an opportunity to contribute to the salvation of the world. For this reason they accept their life of suffering as Jesus Christ accepted his, as Mary Most Holy accepted hers on the day of her purification, and as her faithful and chaste husband St Joseph accepted his.   (19 March 1959)

596 I invite you to offer your illness continually to the Lord, like sweet-smelling incense that rises up into his presence.   (29 July 1959)

597 Your sufferings need no longer be in vain, you can unite them to those of the Crucified One and those of the Virgin, the most innocent of all the creatures. And your life will thus become truly conformed to that of God's Son, King of Sorrows, and be set upon the most secure road to heaven.

(19 March 1959)

598 Behold, in sickness we see the tool offered us by Providence by which we are able to contemplate the sufferings of Christ for his Body, the Church.

(19 March 1959)

599 Jesus' passion shows us just how fruitful suffering can be for the salvation of the world and the sanctification of souls. (19 March 1959)

600 We cannot remain on Mount Tabor, but must follow Jesus to Calvary. (18 March 1968)

601 The purest of joys are to be found everywhere; but we will never want for thorns. Each one of us has their own cross to carry. (13 November 1958)

602 The point of departure for the way to Calvary is the agony in Gethsemane. (6 April 1961)

603 What we begin in triumph at the doors of Jerusalem finishes on the fatal hill of Calvary.

(19 March 1961)

604 Christ's Cross embraces the entire human family. For those who have not been faithful, it is a sign of pardon; for those who have suffered and suffered because they wished to remain united with Christ, it is

a comfort beyond words; and for those who have striven
to make their lives reflect ever more completely the
light of the Saviour, it is a source of great joy.

(13 February 1963)

605 The Cross is the poetry that lies at the heart of
life. Through the Cross we are able to welcome all the
situations in which we find ourselves, our obligations,
and the trials we never lack, with the smile of
supernatural understanding and serenity.

(13 November 1958)

606 We know that through the Cross we can look
into the future with trust.   (13 February 1960)

607 Without sacrifice nothing can be done. Without
the Cross there is no victory.   (29 August 1962)

608 Your life is formed in the image of Christ's own
life, and, although you are free to enjoy certain lawful
amusements, you must never forget the Cross.

(7 March 1962)

609 Love your cross and carry it well, small or great
though it be, in union with the Divine Redeemer.

(18 March 1962)

610 I know very well that you too have your crosses
to carry. For Jesus' carrying of his cross is the most
beautiful image we have of his life, and of our own
lives in the most holy Trinity. Let us carry our crosses
together with honour, and we will know beauty and
joy.   (1 January 1955)

611 Let us not allow ourselves to be fooled, deluded, or made blind: the Cross is the only hope of salvation, always. (3 April 1960)

612 Human life is littered with crosses and sacrifices: it is impossible to remove them. If we accept our crosses in the light of the most holy Trinity then life becomes most wonderful. (1 January 1955)

613 Trials, far from diminishing the flame of faith in the spirit, revive it in a most extraordinary way. (28 December 1958)

614 We are certain that for those who follow Christ not a single tear or sigh, nor moment's worry is ever in vain. All will be of the greatest value for our heavenly glory. (8 March 1961)

615 For those who know how to suffer in the Christian spirit and are sustained by the example of the Mother of God, nothing is ever in vain. (17 August 1958)

616 The Lord accompanies us when we are suffering or in sorrow. When the light of Christ and his peace dwell in our hearts, then all begins well and ends well: weeping turns into joy, humiliation into triumph, and sorrow into glory. (6 April 1960)

617 O most admirable wisdom of God, which knows how to bring about the plans of his infinite mercy concerning us his poor creatures to fulfilment, even through the severest of trials. (28 December 1958)

TEMPTATION

Be clear-headed, be watchful.
Like a roaring lion your adversary the devil
prowls around,
looking for someone to devour.

(1 Pet 5:8)

618 Human history is a fabric woven of weaknesses.
(24 April 1955)

619 Even the world of today is run by gold. It seeks after riches, the goods of the earth, amusements, and money. (11 July 1962)

620 When money is sought with an insatiable voracity, with a desire for worldly glory, with polluted and far from pure pleasures, then arrogant divisions between the classes perpetuate and amplify the discomfort and sadness of the spirit. (29 May 1955)

621 At the bottom of the modern heresy is the denial of original sin. (26 July 1963)

622 I must keep my wits about me and then be prudent, for the devil is more cunning than I.
(*JS*, 31 August 1898)

623 We can observe Satan, in every moment, whispering into the ear of every person: 'See how utterly fascinating are the desires of life, the desires that arise but cannot be satisfied, and how alluring is the love of honours, of glory, and of having yourself affirmed. See:

all of this can be yours, all that you see before you: the fields, the heights, the energies of the earth, if only you will kneel before me and adore me.' We must be ready with our response, as was Jesus: 'Leave me. What you propose would make the Christian unworthy of Christ.' (6 June 1960)

624 The enemy of good tries to overturn the order that God has put in place. He knows how to make use of all weapons: from a despising of the eternal laws, almost as if they were superstitions of the ignorant, to the most narrow-minded spiritual apathy; from the disordered emphasis on personal interests to the most simplistic and intractable demagogy; from the temptation to solitude to intellectual pride and dictatorial intolerance. (6 April 1961)

625 As the night grows darker we must keep awake; we must learn to recognise the deceits of those who are God's enemies before they are ours, and to prepare to defend Christian principles in every way, since they are now and always the breastplate of true justice. (23 December 1958)

626 Satan, like a roaring lion searches for those he can entice and lead to perdition. But wherever there is a light, and grace, the Lord illuminates and sustains us through danger, he protects us and teaches us the path of salvation. (25 July 1959)

627 There is never a lack of occasions to fight the good fight. Let us always be determined to emerge victorious. (4 April 1962)

628 We must learn to feel God's presence and to find him everywhere and at every moment, and so repel the devil and keep him at a distance. (25 July 1959)

629 Christianity without the Cross, without suffering, and without the assaults of the evil one, would not make any sense. (10 November 1959)

630 The good Christian knows that without the Cross, tribulations, and spiritual struggle it is difficult to fight the enemy of the light who is tireless, cunning, and a deceiver. (23 November 1955)

631 Let us fight to our last breath against the temptations of this age in order to ensure the health of our own souls and of those who are dear to us. (23 November 1955)

632 O Mary Immaculate, star of the morning, who disperses the darkness of the deepest night, we turn to you with the utmost trust. Free our feet from all the many seductions that a worldly way of living exposes us to; sustain our vigour not only in youth but in every age, exposed equally as they are to the temptations of the evil one. (8 December 1960)

DEATH

I am the resurrection and the life.
Those who believe in me,
even though they die, will live,
and everyone who lives and believes in me
will never die.

(Jn 11:25-26)

633 The earth, naturally, has its charms: but they pass by and disappear. (30 May 1962)

634 To live long like a vigorous and immovable tree facing all the winds and tempests, to be cut like a delicate spring flower, or to be dragged away like the flimsy rushes that live along a river's bank: these images touch on something essential in the mystery of life, which is sacred for each mortal creature.

(18 January 1958)

635 Our life here below is not destined to go on for ever. We must of course be always ready to respond to the Father's call. (12 March 1961)

636 It is an indisputable truth that we will all one day receive a visit from sister death. She can sometimes make her appearance in a rather sudden and unexpected way. Yet if our tree has yielded its fruits, if our mission has ended well, in conformity with God's will, then we can remain tranquil and unperturbed.

(8 March 1961)

637 The soul which is nearing the end of its voyage, prefers to remain silent and confident in the Lord.

(10 August 1953)

638 If, at the end of our journey, when the Angel of the Lord announces to us that our journey is finished, the door of time closes, and at the very same instant the door of eternity swings open. And so begins true life, without sorrow, without tears, without sunset. In the eternal light and joy of God.

(15 November 1961)

639 We are all subject to the common laws that bind us all. We will die. But we know well that when we die the curtain of the new life will be raised.

(1 March 1963)

640 Though we might have performed miracles while on earth, when we are called to enter heaven we will not be able to ascend our blessed throne unless we each carry our own cross.   (20 November 1961)

641 When death touches the faithful soul the thorns disappear and its song breaks out in the light of God, more open, and more joyful in the feast of the eternal heavens.   (17 November 1957)

642 One day we will have to leave this earthly life. When an old person is dying, full of a life's experiences and bearing the marks of a hard-fought existence and all the troubles they lived through, how beautiful, how sweet it is to remember our Mother. (7 August 1960)

643 During the last day of our earthly life, which is also the first day of our everlasting life, how immensely sweet and welcome it will be to turn to our most merciful Mother, and to have her close in that solemn hour.   (21 November 1962)

644 The worker leaves at the end of the day, but the field will not want for labourers.   (8 March 1961)

645 So let us continue moving slowly towards him, as if he stood waiting with outstretched arms.

(*JS*, 11 August 1961)

646 Death may be close at hand, and what if my lamp were found empty?   (*JS*, 29 August 1903)

647 My Lord Jesus, in whatever year you may call me, may I be found with my lamp full of oil, lest you cast me out into the shadow of death.

(*JS*, 31 December 1902)

The
human person
and other people

THE LAW OF LOVE

Live in love,
as Christ loved us
and gave himself up for us,
a fragrant offering and sacrifice to God.

(Eph 5:1-2)

648 To give oneself entirely to others is the most beautiful flower of our lived faith. (10 December 1955)

649 The basis of charity, which is the heritage of Christianity, lies in the sublime fact that all people are bound together in the same Creator Father, the same Redeemer, and the same Mother who was given to all in the culminating moment of the crucifixion.

(13 November 1960)

650 To the duty each person has towards themselves we must add care for others. There is a saying which is widespread but of little value concerning human doings: 'All for one, and one for all.' (22 January 1963)

651 For me giving is a celebration. And how I wish I could give you even more, and spend myself entirely for each one of you! (5 August 1954)

652 Charity is indeed like precious and refined gold. And whoever possesses it, is enriched and made thankful in the measure which it is given. (6 January 1956)

653 Charity begins with the various ways of showing respect and being courteous that make living with others more pleasant. (19 February 1957)

654 We can give ourselves to our neighbour without a great profusion of compliments repeated endlessly, otherwise there can be no simplicity. (9 January 1963)

655 The habitual smile must know how to conceal the inner conflict with selfishness, which is sometimes tremendous, and when need arises show the victory of the soul over the temptations of the senses of pride, so that my better side may always be shown to God and my neighbour. (*JS*, 10 August 1914)

656 A Christian heart cannot harbour hatred. (18 January 1962)

657 When anxiety and distress keep our wounds open, charity imposes a very precise obligation on us: friendship, esteem, mutual respect; a proper inner attitude, a dialogue that remains open, a forgiveness that makes no exceptions, and a reconciliation that must take place day after day, hour after hour, over the ruins of egoism and incomprehension. (22 November 1959)

658 If true charity were to reign then the world would appear very differently. (22 November 1959)

659 If hatred has given us the bitter fruits of death, we must rekindle true Christian love: the only love that can smooth all the roughness, overcome the dangers, and sweeten suffering. (22 November 1959)

660 The world does not change: discipline will always be necessary. I do not mean the discipline administered through blows and with iron, but the discipline of love. (19 March 1951)

661 Charity enlightens, makes holy, and directs through all our lives. (3 January 1955)

662 We must broaden our horizons and grow in generosity, even at the cost of privations and painful sacrifices, spurred on by Christian charity.

(11 May 1961)

663 Charity overcomes all these obstacles. Charity allows true brotherhood and sisterhood, and good intentions to flourish. Charity is the sure precondition for the peace of Christ in our hearts.

(31 January 1962)

664 Charity is always right. (3 March 1957)

665 The golden rule: give with simplicity, be thoughtful when you are in charge, and bear difficulties with joy. (9 January 1963)

666 'Then he poured water into a basin and began to wash the disciples' feet and to wipe them with the towel that was tied around him.' (Jn 13:5) More than the gesture itself, it is the spirit in which it was done that counts. Every order, every exercise of authority, is a form of service. (11 April 1963)

667 Now it is the hour of mercy, the hour of revenge and bloody rivalry is past. (10 May 1963)

668 Be indulgent towards weakness, tolerate it, remain silent, hide it, and excuse it. (22 June 1958)

669 We must learn from him not to complain, not to get angry, and not to lose our temper with anyone, and not to nurse in our hearts any dislike for those we believe have injured us, but to have compassion for one another; and we must love everyone. You understand what I mean? Everyone, even those who hurt, or have hurt us; we must *forgive*, and pray for them too. Perhaps in God's eyes they are better than we are. (*JS*, 16 January 1901)

670 When our minds are turned to Jesus and Mary it is impossible not to feel well disposed to one's neighbour, rather than cantankerous and ill-disposed to love them. (3 September 1960)

671 The salvation we hope for is primarily the fruit of a great outpouring of charity. We refer to that Christian charity which sums up the entire Gospel. That charity which is always ready to spend itself in the interest of others and which is the surest remedy against worldly pride and immoderate self-esteem. St Paul the Apostle described the characteristics of this virtue when he said: 'Charity is patient, is kind; is not self-seeking; bears with all things, endures all things' (1 Cor 13:4-7). (26 April 1959)

672 Scrupulously avoid as much as a word or a thought against your brother or sister. Hide it, remain silent, and remedy it if you can. (*JS*, 1899)

673 Hands that are used to helping the poor exercise goodness, gentleness, and honesty always and everywhere. (1 December 1955)

674 The whole of the Church's social teaching can be summed up in the following demand of the law of charity: give and give yourself. (3 June 1962)

675 The balm of charity is like the oriental nard which is celebrated in the Scriptures and whose perfume impregnates the hands of whoever touches it, and their whole person. (26 June 1959)

676 Be apostles of charity in your thoughts and in the expression on your face, in word and in deed. Go to whoever is in need and suffers in silence.

(2 June 1962)

677 Let it be love that sustains and gives strength to your spirit: love of your family, of the Church, and of your country; a love that spurs you on to comfort others and almost makes you forget yourself; a love that accompanies you in your strivings to give glory to God and do good to others. (1 March 1959)

678 Love always, love all, love in every circumstance. Even if you find something to condemn about a person, you must still love them. (18 June 1962)

679 Charity is the essence of holiness.

(26 May 1960)

LIVING TOGETHER

And be kind to one another,
tender-hearted, forgiving one another,
as God in Christ has forgiven you.

(Eph 4:32)

680 Christ taught us to be just, to be meek and humble of heart, and to be brothers and sisters, brothers and sisters in the true sense of the word.

(10 January 1959)

681 There is glory enough in these great schemes merely through having had the desire to cooperate in them. (31 January 1960)

682 Enthusiasm is a burning torch that is passed from hand to hand, and must burn ever more brightly.

(13 May 1962)

683 How important it is for you to have faith in yourselves! Avoiding of course the subtle dangers of egoistic individualism, which isolates us and paralyses our every effort. (19 June 1961)

684 Everything that tends to bring people together and inclines them to work for the good of their brothers and sisters is particularly worthy of respect and encouragement. (12 April 1960)

685 Solidarity in misfortune, both Christian and human, is the flower of true Gospel brotherhood and sisterhood. (27 October 1956)

686 Life is a vocation. Only when it is lived as such, only when we are fully aware of life's true nature, can we discover where real satisfaction lies – the secret of interior peace and edification of our neighbour.

(14 July 1961)

687 To find true fulfilment as a human person we must, before anything else, be at peace with ourselves, with our conscience, and most importantly with the Lord. This is true for everyone.   (3 March 1963)

688 We are all aware that we have been entrusted with certain responsibilities. For scientists – as for all people of good will and clear understanding – this awareness will provide a great incentive to work well and with a certain urgency, to act carefully and in the spirit of the apostolate.   (8 December 1959)

689 Discipline is the foundation of individual and social order. Understood correctly and lived wisely it is an expression of harmony, beauty, and generosity.

(13 June 1962)

690 The uses and abuses of the 'rights of the road' do unavoidably involve the mystery of life and death. They also involve the responsibility of everyone who makes use of them. This is a responsibility that no one can avoid.   (9 August 1961)

691 The blood which covers our roads cries to heaven for mercy because of the many precious human lives, the young promising lives, that were uselessly and heedlessly cut short.   (9 August 1961)

692 It is a crime against justice and humanity to destroy or disperse the goods which are indispensable for the survival of the human person. (15 May 1961)

693 To know one another means to love one another; to be united means to progress and to build up. (18 June 1962)

694 Each one of you ought to be able to say: 'I have not ploughed furrows of division and distrust, nor have I saddened immortal souls through my suspicions and fears. I have been open, trustworthy, and trusting. Even those who do not share my ideals have received my sympathy as a brother or sister, so that I might not impede the great plan of Providence when, in its time, it comes to fulfilment.
(22 November 1963)

695 Do not worry about any of the senseless things they might say. Continue on your path. But should they ever be right, and you wrong, turn around immediately. (*JS*, 1911)

696 To know how to forgive, and to forgive from the heart. This is the secret of sweetness and of peace.
(15 September 1958)

697 The mercifulness which is practised between brothers and sisters is the image and the reflection of God's mercifulness towards humanity.
(10 May 1963)

698 Our attitude towards those who persecute, oppress, and kill can only be that of immense pity and compassion. (8 December 1956)

699 When anyone turns to God with a humbled and contrite heart, when they know how to forgive the wrong that has been done them, they are assuredly preparing themselves to receive the Lord's embrace.

(22 July 1961)

700 Patience is like God's touch of blessing and tenderness on everyone. (3 April 1963)

701 Sometimes there are those who believe that they can, in various ways, solve the ordinary problems and questions of our existence. They go about achieving this in a complicated and difficult way, forgetting that a little patience is all that is required to put everything in perfect order and restore calmness and serenity.

(3 April 1963)

702 Be patient. Know how to wait. Then what is in your heart will be visible on our face and all doors will be opened to you; you will win the esteem and affection of all and will be able to sow the seed of the Gospel everywhere. (20 May 1960)

GOODNESS

Do not be overcome by evil,
but overcome evil with good.
(Rom 12:21)

703 There is no knowledge, there are no riches, there is no human strength which equal the value of goodness: sweet, amiable, and patient.

(9 November 1956)

704 The world has need of goodness. The Lord came on the earth to teach it to us. Goodness is sacrifice, obedience, patience, and discipline of the spirit. (25 September 1962)

705 Goodness triumphs in every instance and in all places. (7 November 1962)

706 It is an error to believe that goodness is a small virtue. It is a great virtue, because it implies mastery of oneself, personal disinterestedness, a fervent search for justice, and it is an expression of brotherly charity and the splendour of the same. It is the touch of divine and human perfection in the grace of Jesus.

(9 November 1956)

707 Sweet silence without any hardness, well-intended words inspired by mercifulness and indulgence with the aim of doing good, will be more effective than any proclamations you may make, including those made in confidence.

(*JS*, 13 December 1947)

708 Spread a fragrant oil of sweetness over the sores of humanity. (*JS*, 13 August 1961)

709 Anyone who really tries to be good will suffer humiliation and opposition. But they will always prevail in the end, because goodness is love, and love conquers all.

710 Learning to see with the eyes of our heart is the best way to understand our heart and be in touch with it, and to avoid the temptation of paying too much of the wrong kind of attention and so being deceived by it. (26 July 1953)

711 If you do good, that is, if you are good, you will encounter happy faces everywhere.
(9 November 1956)

PEACE

Peace I leave with you; my peace I give to you.
I do not give to you
as the world gives.
Do not let your hearts be troubled,
and do not let them be afraid.

(Jn 14:27)

712 Among all the good things of life and in the history of humankind, among all the things enjoyed by individuals, families, and peoples, peace is the most precious and important. (22 December 1962)

713 There can be no doubt that some kind of asceticism – some kind of training aimed at helping us to find peace with God, first of all, and then with our neighbours and ourselves – is necessary.

(19 June 1960)

714 Peace with God comes through the fulfilment of his will. Peace with other people comes through the respecting of the rights of every person, because each human person is marked with the splendour of the most high. (13 April 1963)

715 The olive branch of peace no longer shines in our thoughts; the firebrands of war blaze there instead.

(29 June 1959)

716 Indeed, there will be no true peace on earth while those who dwell upon it keep God firmly excluded from their desires and purposes, and while the spirit of violence persists. (15 September 1953)

717 War is the enemy of humankind, it is contrary to the principles of the Gospel, and it always and everywhere leads to irreparable grief and ruin.

(12 June 1955)

718 There has already been enough warfare among people! Too many youths in the flower of life have shed their blood already! Legions of the dead, all fallen in battle, dwell within this earth of ours. Their stern voices urge us all to return at once to harmony, unity, and a just peace.

(29 June 1959)

719 The olive branch is a symbol of the peace that our Lord has promised us. It is the peace that we learn about in his teachings of gentleness, grace, and forgiveness.

(7 April 1963)

720 We are made not for war but for peace. We must constantly strive to live peaceful lives and to train our energies in its spirit.

(11 September 1953)

721 If people are often unable to find real peace, they can merit it to certain extent through faithfulness in keeping the moral law. Care for the moral law allows all the seeds of goodness that God sowed in the human heart to germinate and grow.

(24 December 1961)

722 Peace in families, where the spouses collaborate with the Lord in the transmission of life, and the children grow like olive shoots around the table.

(13 April 1963)

723 Life is a vocation. Only when it is lived as such, only when we are fully aware of life's true nature, can we discover where real satisfaction lies, the secret of interior peace and edification of our neighbour.

(14 July 1961)

724 Charity is peace, and peace means prosperity, while war and the war-like spirit lead to tremendous disasters, always. (10 September 1961)

725 Peace is nourished through patience and trust in Our Lord. (8 July 1956)

726 Our response to the difficulties and storms of life must always be the calm of the Gospel.

(8 July 1956)

727 Where peace is found, Paradise brushes across the earth. (1 April 1962)

WITNESS

Let your light shine before others,
so that they may see your good works
and give thanks to your Father
who is in heaven.

(Mt 5:16)

728 The most important witness required of Christians is unselfishness, uprightness, and sincerity.

(5 January 1962)

729 I am a Christian: this ancient word resounds with a new force. The word no longer requires, as it did in the first centuries of Christianity, that anyone claiming to be described by it give witness through the shedding of blood. What it does ask is persistent, lived, and conscious faithfulness to one's own ideals, one's own Christian vocation, and to the teaching of the Church. (17 June 1962)

730 Every Christian must be convinced that their first and fundamental duty is to be a witness to the truth in which they believe and to the grace that has transformed them. (28 November 1959)

731 The cry of the blind man in the Gospel, 'Lord, let me see again' (Mk 10:51), rises from the lips of the many who are spiritually blind today. Such people perhaps need nothing more from one of their brothers or sisters than a little light they can trust to allow them to walk side by side in the light of truth and love. Many believe that they see clearly, but in truth their spirits and hearts are far from God, plunged in a spiritual night that is far worse than mere physical darkness. May you attract them and draw them after you through your example. (1 October 1959)

732 Carry the goodness, sweetness, and light of Our Lord with you always and everywhere you go.
(23 August 1961)

733 We are all called to walk with Jesus, but that does not in any way mean that we are to leave our material duties unfulfilled, or to neglect the advantages derived from a more elevated way of life that we enjoy, since, in fact, through our relation with Jesus we are called upon to permeate relations between individuals, families, and nations with his heavenly light.
(21 January 1962)

734 In the social field, as in all other areas that concern our living together as human beings, Catholics are aware of the truth that they possess.
(13 May 1962)

735 Let us be an active presence, intelligent and wide-awake when faced by the innumerable problems posed by life today – able to interpret these problems in terms of the eternal truth as reflected in time.
(18 October 1959)

736 Be generous and committed in your work and your apostolic labours, so that the Reign of the Lord Christ might expand throughout the whole world bringing happiness. (26 February 1961)

737 May it be your constant effort to profit from all the opportunities that are offered to you, so that you may redeem the time. (2 June 1962)

APOSTOLATE

What I say to you in the dark,
tell in the light;
and what you hear whispered,
proclaim from the housetops.

(Mt 10:27)

738 Courtesy: the first form of charity and true apostolate. (18 April 1957)

739 The first requirement of the apostolate: a heart detached from the fleeting consolations of earthly life, clear of scheming and worldly interests, free from useless vanities. (5 January 1962)

740 It is not sufficient to live in conformity to Christian teaching and then to run and hide away, and claim that you have fulfilled your task. It is not enough, it is not enough. The Lord desired, and desires, the salvation of all. (22 January 1963)

741 If you wish to dedicate yourself to caring for others you must first be sure of your own growth. (13 March 1963)

742 The spirit that must animate Christians in their apostolic action: a free heart, purity of intention, and generous charity. (5 January 1962)

743 We are all on a journey, and on this journey we are at the service of Jesus, of his Gospel, and the holy Church. Each person has their place, and their appointed time. Those who serve in the Church change, but the Church itself is immortal.

(14 December 1955)

744 The apostle lives in peace, and spreads that peace all around. (13 May 1961)

745 We can never escape the question of mission. The whole question is, simply, one of Catholicism itself, since for those who have been purified in the baptismal font there is no distinction between the profession of faith and the exercise of the apostolate.

(13 August 1957)

746 The apostolate is not a human enterprise with temporal aims, but a divine enterprise, entirely supernatural and simple in its origins and its ends.

(13 May 1961)

747 Anyone who is intimately united with God and seeks for him alone in all things, will of necessity experience the flame of apostolic charity bursting forth.

(16 August 1962)

748 The apostle of Christ, who lives in the light of God, does not give in to feverish agitation or discouragement when confronted with difficulties. With their eyes fixed on eternity the apostle progressively acquires a serene comprehension of the value and of the limits of every activity that unfolds in the world of time here below. (13 May 1961)

749 Apostles look to the good, and for this reason they resolve to bring it forth all around them, even where it is still in seed. (17 February 1962)

750 The activities and forms of apostolate can be very diverse, but the grace that inspires it, perfects it, causes it to first appear and then to grow, just as the morning dew and life-giving sun makes the flowers come forth from the earth, is one. (16 October 1960)

751 It is of course necessary to know and to understand the value of all the things among which we live. But the heart must remain free, anchored with a peaceful security to Christ's divine promises and to a supernatural vision of life and of the world.

(5 January 1962)

752 Our task: to be concerned for others, and especially for those who are far off in the darkness of error and deceit that violence forces upon them.

(13 July 1959).

753 It is always possible to fulfil the apostolate of prayer, for this is accessible to all, and it is irreplaceable in the economy of grace. (4 June 1962)

754 Our apostolate will be fruitful if we know how to turn ourselves into docile instruments of God's grace, instruments that do not seek the passing words of human praise and affirmation but prepare a way for the Lord to pass along. (6 June 1961)

755 With five loaves of bread and two fishes Jesus fed the multitude; he knows how to use your contribution to the apostolate, however small, in order to work wonders. (29 September 1960)

756 We may labour greatly, but it is not always given to us to see the fruits of our labours. We must learn to be patient, as Jesus taught us, as befits anyone who lives by Providence.　　　　(19 August 1953)

757 We are not responsible for success. The only consolation for our inner peace is to know that Jesus Christ is far more interested in the salvation of souls than we are. He desires to save them through our collaboration, but in the final analysis it is grace that saves, and grace is never wanting at the right moment.
　　　　(*JS*, 19 October 1940)

758 The apostle does not pursue their own personal preoccupations, nor seek their own glory, but labours for things which are far-off and everlasting, content to please God alone and to bring souls, possibly all souls, to God's merciful love.　　　　(20 January 1963)

759 Kindness and courtesy, maturity of judgement, prompt obedience, burning charity: in these qualities lies the secret of true and enduring efficiency in the apostolate. They form the basis for the development of every worthy enterprise, and are blessed by God.
　　　　(10 December 1961)

760 The urgent need to succeed may well hide a deceitful desire to appear well before others. Such a need cannot easily be reconciled with the action of Providence, which sows calm, trust, and due measure, and would teach us about those same qualities.
　　　　(5 January 1962)

761 Continue on your journey with joy. Be aware of the great opportunities you have to do good. Do good with serenity and courage. Be the leaven that is destined to make the mass rise.　　　　(2 June 1962)

In the
light of God

JOURNEYING TOWARDS
OUR HOMELAND

For here we have no lasting city,
but we are looking for the city that is to come.

(Heb 13:14)

762 It is right to remember that we are not made for this earth. (16 August 1961)

763 Humankind's destiny lies in seeking their heavenly homeland. (26 July 1953)

764 All human activity, from the highest and most praiseworthy to the more mundane, transcends a merely horizontal and earthly dimension. Everything we do is coloured by the deep-seated human desire to journey towards the City of God. (17 October 1959)

765 The world will pass away. Being impermanent, it often cannot comprehend the things of above, indeed, it often mocks them. But we know in what our true glory lies. (14 June 1961)

766 Here below we are pilgrims, and while our passage may be long or short, it has one sure aim. Let us aim to enter into joy, not punishment.

(7 November 1962)

767 I am a pilgrim here on earth. I look to heaven as my goal, my homeland, my dwelling place. O heaven, you are so beautiful, and you are for me! In all difficulties, bitterness, and discouragements this shall be my consolation: to open my heart to this blessed hope, look to heaven and think of paradise.

(*JS*, February 1900)

768 The way to heaven is to take up the cross with patience, love, and joy. (17 May 1961)

769 We must always walk on, continue on our way, and surmount any obstacle: our feet on the earth, but our gaze continually directed towards heaven.
(2 March 1960)

770 The Christian lives on the earth, but looks to heaven. Life here below, then, is only preparation, trial, and waiting: and for those who were able to remain faithful to the Lord though surrounded by temptations and the disbelief of the world, there will be paradise and joy and the eternal prize. (25 September 1960)

771 Our lives lived in time are always a journey, a crossing. Life gives the opportunity to acquire the qualities that will help us attain salvation and true life, life that will never end. The Divine Redeemer became human and came on this earth to teach us how to act, to obey, and to win the eternal prize.
(21 January 1962)

772 Even though we may be a good way distant from the goal, this does not justify inertia, indifference, or pessimism; rather, it must stimulate our energies.
(3 October 1953)

773 For the good Christian life, even if it leads us through troubles and painful difficulties, is always a foretaste of heaven. (17 February 1957)

774 The just long for Paradise, but their faces, here in this exile, reflect something of that eternal and blessed light which has been promised to the children of God. (2 August 1955)

775 As the years pass so all the different horizons seem to merge into one, while also filling with clarity and a great peace. A good Christian must learn to distinguish those doors which, at the end of their earthly journey, will open onto eternal life.

(8 July 1961)

GLORY

He will wipe every tear from their eyes.
Death will be no more;
mourning and crying and pain
will be no more,
for the first things have passed away
(Rev 21:4)

776 We are not created for this earth, not to be covered by abandonment and oblivion, but for another life, one which has no troubles and is without end. If this is not a vibrant certainty, then existence is gloomy, dark, and deprived of hope   (9 September 1962)

777 At the end of our lives we will come to the gates through which we are able to enter into joy without end. These gates open only for those who are innocent or those who have practised penance. Innocence and penance.   (2 March 1960)

778 We must keep alive within us the thought of heaven, and remember that for the prize that awaits us in heaven, every act has been recorded, no tear is lost, and no interior suffering has been forgotten.
(30 May 1962)

779 Let us think of the paradise that awaits us, let us think often of the joy that there is up above, and let us learn how to bear the sufferings and make holy the sacrifices that present conditions impose on us.
(8 April 1962)

780 When life's difficulties, the hardness of our duties, our weariness, our being misunderstood, or any crises we may be experiencing, threaten our serenity, may the thought of the joy which the Lord is preparing in heaven for his good and faithful servants give us strength and renewed courage.   (5 September 1959)

781 I am standing ready to cross to the other side. The prolonging of my sojourn amongst you, my good children, will certainly give me joy, but I do not ask to live for a minute over the measure of time that Providence has assigned to me.   (25 November 1957)

782 The centuries go on and on. This is certain: their consummation will usher in the eternal glory of Christ, the Son of God, and all those who had faith in him.

783 So we continue along our earthly pilgrimage, remaining united to the Lord; and we will, when he calls us to the heavenly homeland, have the joy of reaching the door of certain salvation and the peace that cannot be disturbed.   (31 December 1961)

784 The Lord has placed us on the earth to serve him in making his love a reality. And so the great and everlasting triumphs of glory are being prepared for us: infinite peace, sweetness and goodness.

(18 July 1962)

785 In the serene light of God we will be united forever with those whom we loved here below and those for whom we have mourned.   (20 March 1960)

786 What is life worth if we are only concerned with appearances? Comfort does not come in through the eyes, but through the heart. Our heart follows the great and luminous spirit to the land of true life – and our gaze must be fixed on that land, a land where the light never fades. (17 October 1958)

Testament of
the heart

THE LAST PRAYER OF POPE JOHN

This bed is an altar. The altar has need of a victim: Here am I; I am ready. I offer my life for the Church, the continuation of the Ecumenical Council, the peace of the world, and the union of Christians.

The secret of my ministry lies in that crucifix you see opposite my bed. He watches over me and I speak with him. During the long and frequent nightly conversations, the redemption of the world has never appeared to be more urgent than it is now. I have other sheep that do not belong to this fold.

Those open arms declare that he died for all, for all. No one is denied his love, his pardon.

It is the *unum sint* ['that all may be one': John 10:16] that Christ particularly wished to leave to his Church as his testimony. It is therefore the task of the Pope and the bishops to enable the clergy and the people to become holy, to foster the union of all Christians, and to advance the conversion of the world.

I had the great grace to be born into a Christian family, modest, and poor, but with the fear of God; and to be called to the priesthood. Since I was a child, I have never thought of anything else, I have never had any other ambition.

Along the way I have met holy priests and good superiors. All helped me and loved me. I have received a lot of encouragement. For my part, I'm not aware of having offended anyone, but if I have, I beg their forgiveness; and if you know anyone who has not been edified by my attitudes or actions, ask them to have compassion on me and to forgive me.

In this last hour I feel calm and sure that my Lord, in his mercy, will not reject me. Unworthy though I am, I wanted to serve him, and I have done my best to pay homage to truth, justice, charity, and the *cor mitis et humilis* ['gentle and humble heart': cf Mt 11:29] of the Gospel.

My earthly day is drawing to a close. But Christ lives on and the Church continues his work. Souls, souls. *Ut unum sint*! *Ut unum sint*!

From a text synthesising the contributions of
many witnesses.

INDEX

PADRE PIO

Words of Light

An anthology of thoughts from
Padre Pio's Letters

A great number of books have been written on the life and works of Padre Pio, but this is not a book about what others think or say about him – here he speaks himself – thoughts, excerpts, counsels and recollections culled from his own writings.

Words of Light is a collection of the most important parts of Padre Pio's correspondence, of the moments that reveal his soul, his asceticism and his mystical life. The letters are the faithful mirror of his soul and they reflect his prayer life, love and suffering.

The selected passages preceded by a short outline of his life, have been arranged in thirteen chapters with a brief introduction highlighting the contents and the central idea of each chapter and the texts that follow are structured around it.

ISBN 085439 600 4   204 pp   £9.99